All Enlisted

A Mormon Missionary in Austria

During the Vietnam Era

by

Roderick Saxey, MD

Published by Haus Sachse Enterprises, Inc.

Copyright 2013, Roderick Saxey, MD

And he said unto them, Go ye into all the world,
and preach the gospel to every creature.

Mark 16:15

*****

We are all enlisted till the conflict is o'er.
Happy are we! Happy are we!

LDS Hymn #250

*****

By this shall all men know that ye are my disciples,
if ye have love one to another.

John 13:35

Missionaries of the Church of Jesus Christ of Latter-day Saints recite the following scripture every morning before starting their work:

Now behold, a marvelous work
is about to come forth
among the children of men.
Therefore, O ye that embark in the service of God,
see that ye serve him
with all your heart, might, mind and strength,
that ye may stand blameless before God at the last day.
Therefore, if ye have desires to serve God
ye are called to the work;
For behold the field is white already to harvest;
and lo, he that thrusteth in his sickle with his might,
the same layeth up in store that he perisheth not,
but bringeth salvation to his soul.
And faith, hope, charity and love,
with an eye single to the glory of God,
qualify him for the work.
Remember faith, virtue, knowledge, temperance, patience,
brotherly kindness, godliness, charity, humility, diligence.
Ask, and ye shall receive;
knock, and it shall be opened unto you.
Amen.

D&C 4

*****

For my children and grandchildren
and for all who go to war.

*****

Foreword

We are molded by the events of those years when we "come of age," whether the Great Depression, World War II, Vietnam, or any of the other periods remembered by our parents, peers, and progeny. For young men and for many young women in the Church of Jesus Christ of Latter-day Saints, one of the most important such events is serving a two-year mission, often in a foreign land speaking a foreign language. At some point we all have to put in perspective the spirit of that time, those events, and our roles in them. Some do it in reverie, some with psychoanalysts or bar-tenders. I chose the tamer and more durable alternative of the memoir.

This work is based on four sources. My recollections are the bulk of the material and are therefore subject to the limitations of memory, biases of viewpoint, and prejudices of thought that are the common lot of mankind. Apologies to those who remember things differently! Contemporaneous journal entries (*italics*) and letters (Dear . . .) are quoted with minimal editing and have the same limitations mentioned above as well as the age-related limitations of the teenage brains that wrote them. Some journal/letter entries have been combined to decrease redundancy.

Finally, I have used a variety of historical and contemporary news reports and records to fill in details of events, especially what was happening in Vietnam and in America while I was serving in Austria. Those, too, as we have learned to a cynical degree in the modern era, are subject to significant limitations of viewpoint and bias, especially political bias. Those confessions made, what else can be said? We try the best we can.

Although the focus of this memoir is on mission experiences during the Vietnam era, comments are made in the text about events of World War II and other conflicts, both earlier and later, and their effects on individuals and society at large. As elaborated below, these all can be seen as parts of a larger war, one that stretches back before the dawn of creation: to labor for freedom of the soul from sin or for freedom from earthly tyranny are two sides of the same cloth. The threads of history interweave in a complex way and have consequences for subsequent generations. They even extend to the current world dilemmas brought on by the spread of Islamo-fascism, for this too has connections to my little corner of Austria.

Contents

Chapter 1

I was born almost exactly mid-century, a month before the outbreak of the Korean War. In elementary school we had air-raid drills and learned to duck under our desks until the all-clear. A recurrent exercise in school or on the playground was the planning of how we would survive an attack, re-group in the mountains, and fight back against invaders.

Later, in the seventh grade, there was great excitement in our little Yakima Valley town of Sunnyside, Washington, over the capture of a Soviet spy ring that had been operating among us, befriending neighbors, and gathering information about the nearby Hanford nuclear project. Hanford was where the government produced the fuel for our nuclear weapons, including the bomb used on Nagasaki. Such events fired our youthful imaginations and we all daydreamed of spies. By the time the first James Bond movie, *Dr. No*, came along in 1962 our minds were fully-prepped and ready for adventure.

My family had moved to Sunnyside from Portland, Oregon, before I was two years old so that Dad could become the x-ray and laboratory technologist at Valley Memorial Hospital (one suspects the administration was delighted to get two-for-one; Dad was very talented). Sunnyside was a pleasant farm town of about 5,000 people. Thanks to the Santa Rosa irrigation project, the rich volcanic soil of the surrounding fields and orchards produced an abundance of apples, cherries, pears, asparagus, mint, corn, peas, alfalfa, and other crops. There were cattle ranches and dairies, canneries and feed lots. Major events included Ben Snipes Day (in honor of the founding pioneer), Independence Day, Homecoming, and the Toppenish Pow-Wow, a rodeo held on the edge of the Yakima Indian Reservation. Our heroes rode horses, captured bad guys, and wore six-shooters, except for Superman, of course, who didn't need them. Sunnyside was about as typical an example of small-town western America as could be found in the 1950s.

Mom and Dad raised prize-winning German Shepherds and wanted to expand the kennels, so midway through our sojourn there we moved from an old Victorian house on 13th street to a fourteen acre farm just outside of town. Half was planted with asparagus and the other half was pasture. My parents thought big: we eventually had as many as 45 dogs at a time, as well as 65 head of sheep, 4 horses, a dozen steers, assorted cats, chickens, and geese. Beyond the greenery of the valley were rolling hills of sagebrush in every direction, with Mt. Rainier standing as a glistening white sentinel in the west.

Although this was decades before the 24-hour News Cycle, the Saxey and Hall families always followed closely the papers, magazines, radio, and later the television reports to keep up with the news. Our immediate genealogical tree included many newspapermen and other professionals, so the troubles of the world were never far from our thoughts even in a rural setting. We grew up with crises in Berlin, Cuba, Suez, and elsewhere, not to mention the televised remembrances of World War II: *Victory at Sea*, *Churchill Remembers*, and the ongoing parade of war movies such as *The African Queen, The Bridge Over the River Kwai, The Longest Day,* and *The Great Escape.*

Through all of this, whether the play and imagination of children or the real-life news reports and documentaries of adults, there was a constant theme, namely, the eternal struggle of Good versus Evil, of Freedom versus Tyranny. We, of course, were on the side of Good and Freedom, or in other words: Truth, Justice, and the American Way.

And then came Vietnam.

* * * * *

I first became aware of Vietnam on 4 August 1964 when President Johnson addressed the nation about the Gulf of Tonkin incident, a pair of small skirmishes between North Vietnamese gunboats and American ships in international waters near Vietnam. As we heard details of what had happened (many of which were shown later to be incorrect) and our government's response, Dad could only shake his head. Mom asked, "What does that mean?" Dad replied quietly, "it means war."

Because we followed the news so closely, even though a child I remembered the end of the Korean War, as well as the building of the Berlin wall, the Cuban Missile Crisis, and various other conflicts of the Cold War, but Vietnam had the feel of something quantitatively and qualitatively different. That turned out to be true in ways I could not have expected or imagined.

The Vietnam War had its roots in the aftermath of World War II. Mao tse-Tung led his communist followers on a successful conquest of China, with the nationalist forces of Chiang Kai-shek withdrawing to Formosa, now called Taiwan. Ho Chi Min hoped with the help of the Chinese and the Soviet Union to accomplish the same victory in Vietnam, then part of a larger entity called French Indochina which included Laos and Cambodia. He was only partly successful, gaining control of the northern half of the country. The French fought Ho's forces bitterly from 1950 to 1954, but finally acknowledged his victory by signing The Geneva Accords, a treaty which formally recognized the communist government of North Vietnam. The United States and the government of South Vietnam did not sign the Accords, however, and that was the start of our greater involvement there.

Containment was a foreign policy doctrine conceived in Western Europe in the 1920's as a means of dealing with the emerging Soviet Union and was established by President Truman as official American policy toward communism in general. Presumably this meant keeping the communists under control until something happened to change them from their bellicose ways. It was never very clear what it was that could accomplish that. From the communist viewpoint, containment meant they could push, prod, and ever expand, knowing that they kept every gain and that every loss was only temporary.

So it was that the departure of the French from Indochina and the arrival of the Americans meant simply that their enemies were speaking a different language, with little other difference. The "something" that would bring about a successful end to the Cold War was a consistently firm and unified resistance to tyranny in the West combined with internal economic and moral decay within the communist regimes, but that combination of conditions did not mature until Reagan and Thatcher, thirty years later.

For President Eisenhower in the mid-1950s the principle of containment was colored by the great general's apprehension at being involved in a ground war in Asia, the avoidance of which had long been a guiding principle of American military teaching. On the other hand, there was fear that if Vietnam was lost to the communists, Laos, Cambodia, Thailand, and all the rest of Southeast Asia would not be far behind—they would fall like dominoes. The United States had already provided most of the weapons and financing for the unsuccessful French war. Eisenhower decided to continue to help the South Vietnamese with the addition of American military advisors as well as intelligence and other support.

The following years were a time of regrouping, organizing, and politicking for Vietnamese on both sides. A series of international crises early in President Kennedy's term had the net effect of pushing him toward greater efforts in Asia. Though still determined not to deploy ground troops, by 1963 he had increased Eisenhower's 900 advisors to 16,000. For their part, the South Vietnamese during this time period were ineffective and inept in dealing with the threat from the North and more particularly with communist insurgents among them in the South, known as the Viet Cong. A coup against the corrupt South Vietnamese leader, Diem, resulted in his execution and threw the nation into even greater turmoil. In October, 1963, President Kennedy directed that the American presence should begin to wind down, fearing that we could become bogged down in a long and unsuccessful war as the French had been. Then history delivered another of its unexpected twists.

President Kennedy's assassination on 22 November 1963 was announced over the intercom during our 8th grade homeroom class. Reactions among students varied dramatically from hysterical weeping to inappropriate laughter, but most of us were subdued. Though disagreeing with him politically, he was still another person like us with beloved family and friends. I sorrowed for his untimely loss; more importantly, he was the President, the mouthpiece and representative of the nation. A blow to him was a blow to all of us and to the country we loved so much.

Events progressed rapidly. Two days later Mom and Dad and I watched TV news showing Jack Ruby shoot the accused assassin, Lee Harvey Oswald, before he could be tried. As we headed toward the back door to go to the kennel and feed the dogs, Mom commented, "First one of the greatest in the country, then one of the lowest. Next thing, one of us ordinary people in the middle will be shot." Minutes later, a hunter on the other side of our little valley fired a shotgun at some birds. We felt and heard the shot whiz between us and strike the wooden fence by the house, narrowly missing us. We shouted at him to stop, then counted our blessings.

Now installed as president, Lyndon Johnson halted the planned withdrawal from Vietnam, but neither did he significantly increase our involvement at first. He was preoccupied with a variety of social programs including his ill-fated "War on Poverty" which could not previously pass Congress, but now, with the sympathy evoked by Kennedy's assassination, were moved to the front burner. Conditions in Southeast Asia continued to deteriorate.

When the North Vietnamese fired on two of our ships in separate incidents in the Gulf of Tonkin in August, it was time for greater action. President Johnson addressed the nation and Congress passed the Gulf of Tonkin Resolution, which authorized him to use whatever force he deemed necessary in the region. Initially this consisted of greater bombing of enemy positions and cities, but gradually increased to full scale deployment and engagement. By 1969 over 500,000 American troops were in Vietnam.

As we watched the president on TV in 1964 our main concern was for Wayne, my older brother serving in the army in northern Japan, and what this might mean for him. We could not know that my eldest brother, Edward (then attending the University of Washington in Seattle) would be sent there twice, or that my high school class of 1968 would find ourselves coming of age at the height of this long, difficult, and increasingly unpopular war. Members of our class divided along different paths—some went to war, some demonstrated against the war, some hid from the war by fleeing to Canada. And then there were some of us who did none of those things, but went to fight battles of a different sort in a war that involves the whole world and everyone in it, sooner or later.

*****

Our family history demonstrates two contrasting approaches to world upheavals: flight or fight. In 1817, after the father of the German Raile family was killed somewhere in France fighting Napoleon, his wife and children took ship down the Danube to join relatives near Odessa. A generation later, the Keils, fearing their young son would be drafted into the continuing European wars, emigrated from Bavaria to Jerusalem. Our most recent French forebear escaped the French Revolution and fled over the border to Germany. He took the common local name of Faas, lest his enemies pursue him, refusing even to tell his new wife what his real name was. And great-great-grandfather James Henry Hall chose to return AWOL to his Tennessee farm rather than take up arms when drafted by the Union near the end of the Civil War.

But many of our family had the other type of experience. If not plunging headlong into the world's crises like great-grandpa Alfred Saxey, who volunteered for the Kansas infantry at the beginning of the Civil War, they at least were caught up in them. Saxeys, Halls, Tildens, Lords, and their collateral lines participated in all of America's conflicts since the Pilgrims first arrived. Before that we were in the Wars of the Roses, the Battle of Agincourt, the Crusades. Everywhere we look in history, we are there. So imagine the delight I felt in 1961 when I visited grandma and grandpa Saxey in Provo, Utah, was allowed to try on grandpa's Spanish-American War uniform and great-grandpa's Civil War uniform, and had them fit. A year later, grandpa had died and the uniforms were at our house; they did not fit anymore.

Something unexpected happened after that visit to Provo and I wondered later if my grandparents had some influence. Latter-day Saints are usually baptized at age 8, but Mom thought 12 was a better age because that was Christ's age when he was teaching in the temple. My parents decided that, though not quite 12, it was time for me to be baptized anyway, and since I was over the usual age, I would have to have the missionary lessons. After school each week I walked a few blocks downtown to the missionaries' apartment and they taught me about the gospel.

The lessons were vaguely familiar because we had attended church a few times, but many of the details were new. I especially loved the Plan of Salvation, which made so much sense and answered key questions about life and the purpose of it. I also loved the story of the boy prophet, Joseph Smith, who prayed for guidance and was rewarded with a visitation by God, the Father, and His Son, Jesus Christ. Joseph was inspired to translate the *Book of Mormon*, a collection of ancient scriptures similar to the Bible, which testifies of Christ and verifies and clarifies the teachings in the Bible. It was all beautiful, and I loved learning it.

Elder Wanlass and Elder Christensen enjoyed teaching; I realized later that I was a "golden contact". What I could not know at the time was that the lessons they taught and the flannel board illustrations they used were the same I would be using a few years later. I was baptized on 23 December 1961, Joseph Smith's birthday.

Religion was not a preoccupation of everyday life in our household, but it was an important part of our upbringing nonetheless. A picture of Christ in the Garden of Gethsemane hung on the wall, Dad said grace before every meal, Mom taught me to pray when still very young ("Now I lay me down to sleep . . . "), and we attended church at Christmas and Easter. The folks also would occasionally send my brothers and me to Sunday School, and the three of us participated in Boy Scouts. I also went to the Methodists' week-long Summer Bible School each year. Being baptized did not appreciably change this minimal level of church involvement.

Grandpa Hall, Mom's father, took his family to a variety of Protestant denominations through the years, and was always supportive of the local clergy, providing meals and other help which were especially important during The Great Depression. He told his children they could choose what religion they wished, so long as they did not marry a Catholic or a Mormon. His son, Hal, seeing the world in the Merchant Marine, married a charming Mexican Catholic with a large extended family and settled in Mexico City. His daughter, Mom, married a Mormon boy from Utah. Perhaps he should have tried reverse psychology.

Dad's great grandparents had joined the Church of Jesus Christ of Latter-day Saints in London and in Jerusalem, subsequently migrating to Utah. Though born in Provo, most of his childhood was spent in Price, a polyglot eastern Utah mining community of immigrants with a particularly large Greek population. That background, combined with a cosmopolitan feeling within the home and pride for our connection to the Holy Land (his mother was born in Jaffa), contributed to a familial appreciation of other cultures. Among our favorite family foods were "goosai and rice" and "mochshee", which his grandmother had learned from "the Arabs".

Dad attended Brigham Young University in Provo before deciding to move to Portland, Oregon. Among his good friends in Portland was Thomas Y. Emmett, who later became our stake president and eventually the first Portland Temple President. They, as well as several missionaries and home teachers tried over the years to interest Dad's girlfriend, then fiancé, then wife in the restored church. Mom was resistant, preferring to stay close to her Protestant upbringing and not to upset her father more than he already was about his Mormon son-in-law. Dad was quiet, good-natured, and not pushy; peace remained easy; and religion was never a matter of great conflict that I was aware of.

My parents were married in Portland on 25 September 1940, which coincided with Dad's parents' anniversary. Edward was born just after Pearl Harbor during a blackout for fear of Japanese bombers. Wayne was born two years later. Dad worked in the shipyards as a welder during most of the war while Mom worked as an assistant to Dr. Frank Everett, an oral surgeon from Austria. America's wartime industry accomplished great feats. Dad spoke of meeting a challenge to build a "baby flattop", a small aircraft carrier, in only a week.

Since Dad was older, married, had children, and was going to school (at the University of Portland) it came as a surprise when he was drafted in March 1945 into the army, which trained him as an X-ray Technologist. Victory was declared in Europe shortly before they were to ship out, so their commander assembled the company and told them that anyone who was married and wanted to stay stateside and go home early should step forward. Dad suspected this might be the only chance he would ever have to go to Europe and remained in his place.

He was assigned to a hospital in Florence, Italy, a place that remained dear to his heart ever after. He loved art and, in addition to outings to Paris and Rome, spent his free days poking around the city of the Medicis looking for things he had only read about. The highlight of his time there was when he found Michelangelo's David in a warehouse where it had been stored for safe keeping. The warehouse guard came out shouting that GIs weren't allowed and he had to leave. Dad said he would, but wanted just a moment to admire "the greatest statue in the world." The guard asked him if he knew what he was looking at, to which he replied, "Of course." The guard said, "Oh. In that case, come in," and took him on a tour of all the masterpieces that had been hidden there.

Dad's work in the hospital proved useful experience for him professionally, but was enlightening in other ways as well. He had grown up with German in the home and studied it in college, so he understood the German Prisoners of War as they bantered back and forth while working in the yard, complaining about their sergeants and boasting of their rule-breaking exploits. He came to the conclusion that we won the war because they just screwed around more than we did.

After returning from Italy, Dad finished his degree in biochemistry and started medical school at the University of Oregon. I was born during that period into what must have been a very busy household. Years of working two jobs and going to school full-time while raising a family took their toll; Dad decided the schedule was just too hectic and dropped out. A short time later he accepted the hospital job in Sunnyside, where we remained a little over eleven years. It was a great place to be a kid.

The move back to Portland in 1963 did not come as a complete surprise to me—I had seen it in a recurrent dream. One of Dad's medical school friends, a pathologist named Bill Lehman, had asked him repeatedly to come work for him in his laboratory there. Finally the offer was at the right time in our family life, for the older boys were out of the house, I had not yet started high school, and Dad had given up on his dream of building the kennels into a business his sons would want to continue after him.

The folks found a new split level home on two acres between Happy Valley to the north and Sunnyside (Oregon) to the south, not far from Dr. Lehman's home. There were berry farms, pastures, orchards, and woodland all around us, and Dad and Edward built a small kennels for the twenty or so dogs that we kept. Though close to the Lents district of Portland, where Dad had proposed to Mom so many years ago, and an easy commute for Dad to work, it still had the feel of country living.

Chapter 2

After we moved back to Portland I attended Mutual a couple times, but Scouting was not high on the priority list of the 10th Ward leadership at that time and I lost interest. I missed my old Scoutmaster, Brother Ackerman, and besides, was quite proud of the quartermaster and Fort Simcoe Area Council badges on my uniform and did not want to take them off. I remained inactive that year despite the efforts of new friends who also were members of the Church, notably Don Waddell, with whom I became friends in 8th grade Science class. I incidentally discovered to my satisfaction that the schools in Sunnyside were ahead of those in Portland—without any additional effort my grades jumped a full letter, so I looked forward to doing well in high school.

We had a faithful Home Teacher, Clair Cantwell, who came every month and visited with us. (Home Teaching is a program of the Church in which men holding the priesthood visit other members, make sure they are all right, provide help, and deliver short, uplifting messages. In a word, it is "ministering".) Brother Cantwell had a cheery manner and was always encouraging, which were important traits to have since he was also our dentist. Near the end of summer, 1964, he invited me to attend seminary, the early morning religion class taught by the Church for high school students. Arising early enough to attend another class did not appeal to my young sensibilities, so I turned him down.

Bookish by nature, my habit was always to have something with me to read, and selections ranged through a variety of fiction and non-fiction works. The summer of 1965 I realized that I had never read the New Testament, so carried a pocket edition with me as I wandered the fields and woods that surrounded our home. I was moved by the accounts of Christ's life and ministry, and felt the Spirit confirm the testimonies of the Apostles, especially John, as well as those of Luke the physician and of James, the brother of Jesus. There was no doubt in my heart that Jesus was the Christ.

In late August Brother Cantwell repeated his invitation to attend seminary, pointing out that I could still complete the three years which were required for graduation. The invitation was genuine, but he could not hide a certain lack of confidence in its acceptance. I did not understand why I said, "Yes," but the expression of shock and surprise on Brother Cantwell's face alone was enough to make it worthwhile. He stammered a little as he said he would call around to arrange rides; it was short notice.

Those rides turned out to be one of the important ingredients in my personal conversion process. Waddells, Cantwells, Fackrells, and others provided not just rides, but also cheerful socializing, encouragement, and fellowship. The Waddells, who lived nearby on the other side of Happy Valley, offered to take me to church and soon I was going with them to Sunday School, Sacrament Meeting, Priesthood Meeting, and, during the week, to Mutual. From time to time I would join them for Family Home Evening on Monday nights, as well as Sunday evening "firesides", occasional meetings usually featuring only one special speaker or choir. Over the course of the year I went from inactive to fully active, and the testimony I had gained of Jesus Christ grew to a testimony of His restored church as well. The missionary lessons at age 11, it seemed, had been merely seeds which now sprouted.

It so happened that the seminary course of study that year was church history. The Latter-day Saints teach that there was a great apostasy as the original twelve apostles died, and though there were many good and faithful Christians after that time, the priesthood authority to act in God's name had been lost, along with many important doctrinal truths. Those truths, the "fullness of the gospel", and priesthood authority began to be restored when God called Joseph Smith as a prophet in New York in 1820; in 1830 the Church was established anew in our age and has continued to this time.

The *Book of Mormon* is a book of ancient scripture translated by the prophet, similar to the Bible, which testifies of the divinity of Jesus Christ. It also teaches that America is a land of promise for those who love liberty and desire to serve God, that the United States was founded under the influence of the Holy Spirit, and that the framers of the Constitution were placed in their time and place for that purpose. It was necessary to create a nation in which the gospel could be restored and the Church could prosper, events that would have been much more difficult in the setting of an oppressive government and an established state religion. In other words, one of the ways that God guides the destinies of nations is by inspiring people to do good, even at great personal sacrifice, always preserving individual agency. We are free to choose.

Of course, while I was experiencing personal changes and growth, change was occurring with the rest of the family as well. Wayne was discharged home from the army after serving three years in Japan. He said later that the army had offered him a promotion and a bonus if he would re-enlist and accept an assignment to some exotic places in Southeast Asia. He said that if the army wanted to do all that to get him to go there, it was certainly not where he would want to be.

14 February 1966, Portland

Last fall Wayne came back from the army; we were extremely fortunate to get him out, what with the crisis in Viet-Nam and all. He stayed with us for awhile, but then moved to an apartment across town. . . .

Edward graduated last Spring from UW and went to work as a civilian aeronautical engineer at Edward's Air Force Base in California. He was particularly enthusiastic about being able to fly (the Air Force would not accept him for military flight because of his eyesight), but then during training at Edward's he fainted and so was disqualified from that program, which was discouraging for him.

As a sophomore at Clackamas High School, I became interested in religion and started seminary; in order to attend, I have to get up at six a.m.

The war in Viet-Nam is well underway now. There are some 200,000 Americans there. Every day we hear reports of battles in places no one has ever heard of before. Demonstrations against the war, communist riots, demonstrations, etc. are events that take place every day in American streets. . . .

Richard Nixon is the favorite for the Republican nomination in 1968. Mother doesn't like the idea because he has lost twice before. Just the same, I think he is the best choice. No other politician is his superior, unless it could be Everett Dirkson, but he is too old.

In freshman English class in 1965 we all had to give 3-5 minute talks on some subject or other. English was my favorite class and Mr. Anderson was my favorite teacher. Nevertheless, for some unaccountable reason, standing in front of the class caused me to freeze. I could barely stumble and mumble my way through a sentence. It was terrible.

Something remarkable happened over the next couple years. Young people in the church were called upon frequently to give short talks in Sunday School and other meetings, so by the time I was a junior I had had much more experience with public speaking. Mr. Anderson also taught Junior English. This time all went well. In fact, my talk about foreign aid was given during a thunderstorm and there was a loud crack of thunder in the middle of it, causing all the class to jump in their chairs and look at the rattling windows. I looked at the windows too and said something like, "Huh. I didn't know there were any Democrats up there." Everyone laughed and the rest of the talk was delivered uneventfully. As I returned to my seat Mr. Anderson paid me one of the nicest compliments when he whispered to me as I passed, "I'm glad you were the one talking when the thunder pealed."

6 May 1966, Portland

For the first time in my life I have given my testimony. It was at the Seminary Conference here in town. It was odd. I had previously determined that I was not going to bear my testimony, but as I watched the other young men and women and heard their testimonies, I decided what I had come to know inside about the Gospel was more important than any embarrassment I might feel. I resolved that in the future I would do my utmost to live a life like the Lord would want. Although I have not been entirely successful, I will keep on trying . . . .

Clyde and Eudora Waddell were two of the finest people I knew. He led with gentleness and confidence; she kept the household organized and functioning, and was a fine cook to boot. Both had a guileless forthrightness that was thoroughly comforting. Their family consisted of two daughters, Ellen and Arlene, and two sons, Don and Ken. Don became my best friend and I felt warmly welcomed by the whole family. There seemed always to be something going on, whether games, target practicing with our 22s in the backyard, or just hanging around enjoying each other's company. Plus, Don's sisters also happened to be witty, pleasant, and very pretty. Sisters were a new experience for me—even brothers were a little unusual since Edward and Wayne were so much older and had been out of the house for a few years already.

For the Waddells, church, church activities, and the principles of the gospel were an ordinary part of everyday life, as much a commonplace as sleeping at night or eating at mealtime, not oppressive in any way, but simply the context of daily life. To speak of news at church was as usual as news in the nation or in the neighborhood, and there was always news. Church membership had just reached the two million mark, most of whom lived in the western United States.

They were excited that their cousin, Thomas S. Monson, had been made a member of the Quorum of Twelve Apostles only a few years before, in 1963. He was the youngest member of the quorum and Sister Waddell commented, "All he has to do is live and he will be the prophet some day." Her words proved prophetic as well, but Elder Monson and I crossed paths before then, more than once.

David O. McKay was the prophet at the time, that is to say, President of the First Presidency of the Church, the council of three

High Priests who lead the church along with the Quorum of Twelve Apostles, all of whom are sustained as prophets, seers, and revelators. When the President dies, the senior member of the Quorum normally succeeds him. Then in his nineties, President McKay was a distinguished looking man who, even in old age, had thick, wavy, white hair; he looked very much like Grandpa Saxey. President McKay had made progress in ameliorating the hostility which some other Christians had previously had toward the Church through ecumenical and humanitarian outreach, as well as greatly expanding missionary work and developing church leadership outside the United States.

23 May 1966, Portland

The 21st was my sixteenth birthday. The next day I was interviewed by Bishop Wiest to be a Deacon. My parents were not present so we decided to wait two weeks before my ordination (next week is Stake conference). The ordination was performed by him on 29 May 1966. Ordination as a Teacher followed on 31 July. It was absolutely wonderful. I cannot convey the love which I feel for the Waddell family; I look on them as part of my family. One week ago I received my patriarchal blessing; it was a tremendous experience. I only wish my parents would come to church with me.

Patriarchal blessings are inspired blessings given to people, usually in their teens, by a patriarch. There is one patriarch in each stake who has authority to give these blessings, which are regarded as revelations from the Lord revealing His will concerning the recipients. It helps give guidance throughout life, especially during difficult or trying times.

Priesthood is authority to act in God's name, or, in practice, to perform ordinances and other service in the Church. Young men usually receive the Aaronic, or Lesser Priesthood at age 12. Through the teenage years they are given increasing amounts of responsibility as they progress through offices in that priesthood: deacon, teacher, and priest.

Teachers can be assigned as Home Teaching companions to adult men holding the Melchizedek, or Greater Priesthood; my first assignment was with Lee Cantwell, Clair's younger brother. Lee was a tall, skinny man with a great sense of humor. The humor started when he drove up: he had a little Volkswagen beetle and would have to fold and unfold himself as he got into and out of the car. It was a great experience to zip up and down the hills of southeast Portland, visit members, enjoy their company, and pray with them.

A priest can baptize new members and bless the sacrament (communion) bread and water each week, which is then passed to the congregation by the deacons. If someone joins the church or becomes active when older than 12, the process is accelerated until he has reached the age-appropriate office.

6 November 1966, Portland

I was ordained a Priest on 16 October by Brother Waddell. The first time I blessed the sacrament, I got about half-way through the prayer when it occurred to me how important the ordinance was that I was performing—I was in effect filling in for Jesus. I almost did not make it through the last line. This morning I bore my testimony and in it made a prayer that somehow my Mother, who was at this particular meeting, might be baptized.

President Don C. Wood, our Priests' Quorum advisor, was a tall, robust man with a disarming smile and energetic manner. Enthusiasm poured from him and was a hallmark of his talks and lessons. He had been released as president of the Northwestern States Mission a couple years before and, rather than return to Utah, stayed in Portland to work for the Sisters of Providence, heading up their research division (he had a PhD in biochemistry).

His lessons were peppered with inspirational stories drawn from his many experiences. As a graduate student at Cornell he had been instrumental in teaching the gospel to Brother Kim, who joined the Church and took the gospel back to South Korea, where he laid the foundation of a great missionary work there. President Wood's devotion to the restored gospel went back far beyond college days to his youth and childhood.

He told us of his patriarchal blessing and a promise that at times of greatest danger he would hear a voice say, "Thus far shalt thou go and no further." He said he had heard the voice three times. The first was when he was a young marine recruit in training during World War II and they had their first liberty. He went with the others to town and sat with them in a bar. Though his conscience warned him not to go in, he thought simply to keep his friends company with a soda. Then, as the waitress turned to him, he heard the voice, "Thus far shalt thou go and no further." He immediately rose and returned to base.

The value of the warning was even clearer a few months later when on patrol in a Pacific island jungle. He was point—the man in front—when he heard the voice say, "Thus far shalt thou go and no further." He stopped and his unit walked silently past him, assuming that he was due for routine rotation to the rear of the column. The new point man walked only a few yards when he was shot dead by a Japanese sniper. President Wood never told us about the third time he heard the voice.

5 February 1967, Portland

Edward has enlisted in the Navy. In March he will go to Pensacola, Florida, for flight training. He will be a Flight Officer.

The Naval Flight Officer sits in the back seat—perfect vision was not a requirement—and controls navigation, communications, radar, target acquisition, and often weapons delivery itself, especially management of airborne rockets. In other words, he does nearly everything except fly the aircraft. As things turned out, the Navy F-4 Phantom that Edward would fly was the same version he had worked on as an engineer while working at Edwards AFB. His intimate knowledge of its structure and capabilities saved his life and the aircraft on more than one occasion. By temperament and training, Edward was perfectly suited to his assignment, but I doubt he really knew how well suited he was until later.

While my brother was being trained by the Navy, I continued my training in the priesthood. President Wood's lessons in Priesthood Meeting and Sister Wood's lessons in Sunday School continued to inform and delight. Many of his most memorable stories were from his time as Mission President, perhaps because that was so recent. He told how he and his assistants went to Neah Bay on the Olympic Peninsula in the far northwest corner of Washington to open the Makah Indian Reservation to missionary work. They knew that to be accepted they would have to get permission from the Chief. When they arrived they asked who the Chief was and where they could find him. They were directed to Luke Markistun, who lived in back of the tavern he operated.

Luke invited them into his living quarters and President Wood taught about the nature of God. He asked the Chief how he pictured God. Luke leaned back in his chair, put his arms behind his head (he had large, lumberjack arms), and said, "God is a man, strong like me, bronze like Indian." The image was very clear. They taught him about Joseph Smith, the restoration, modern prophets, and about the Book of Mormon. President challenged him to pray about their message and he accepted the challenge. Kneeling together at the Chief's bedside, he asked God if the messages he had heard were true. At the conclusion of the prayer, as President Wood began to rise, he felt the Chief's big hand on his shoulder, holding him down for what seemed like several minutes. When finally they rose, wet spots could be seen where the Chief's eyes had touched the covers. "When Indian prays," he said, "he waits for the answer." Missionaries were welcomed into Neah Bay.

2 April 1967, Portland

Today I heard the testimony of Luke Markistun, Chief of the Makah Indians in Neah Bay, Washington. He is an amazing man. When he was eight he dreamt he was on the steps of a temple when he heard a voice call his name. He turned and saw a white man who led him up the steps. As he went up the steps he heard the music of an angelic choir. Many years later when he first met President Wood, he recognized him at once as the man he saw in his dream, so he listened to his message. Later he heard the choir and saw the tabernacle when he visited Temple Square in Salt Lake City.

President Wood is a great influence on me. As a member of the Youth Missionary Committee, I had a chance to talk to him of the Mission Program, which I have not been very good at. He inspired me greatly and I can't help but feel that something wonderful is going to happen soon.

What happened next turned out to be not so wonderful after all.

8 April 1967, Portland

Yesterday I underwent the terrifying experience of taking a girl to a dance. I didn't dance—I couldn't dance. So we talked; I am afraid it was awfully dull for her. I have sadly neglected a critical part of my education, namely socializing, including dancing. Sister Ward has been pushing me to join the dance festival. Maybe that is the answer to my problem; or it may only make it worse. Life was so much easier when I was just a funny little guy who read too much. . . I talked to Dad about it. He said I should learn to dance.

In fact, I did not learn to dance until fall of 1968 when I went to college and took a class in ballroom dancing, and I never learned it well. But then again, I did not go on many dates either— the prospect was too intimidating. Growing up on a farm with only two much older brothers and no sisters, I never had close friends my own age, and had very little interaction with girls. My best friends were the dogs. They were always ready to play, always eager to please, and always understanding and forgiving. My social clumsiness proved an obstacle for years to come.

16 April 1967, Portland

Last night I had the great privilege of baptizing Lana Jean McFarlane. She is a friend of President Wood's neighbor. Since he is out of town, he asked me to perform the ordinance for him. She is a very nice person and will make a great Mormon. I also went to our Sunday School class party at Don's. For three days before the baptism I fasted two meals a day, and on the day of the baptism I did not eat anything until afterwards, so refreshments at the party were very welcome.

At Sacrament meeting this evening, it was announced that on 1 May the ward will divide to form a new 15th Ward. The old 10th Ward will be the geographically smallest in the state. The division was almost perfect, with roughly equal numbers of members and priesthood bearers in both wards. Brother Waddell is the new Bishop, with Lee Cantwell (my Home Teaching companion) as 1st Counselor, and Ron Thompson as 2nd Counselor.

25 April 1967, Portland

Dad was called as 1st Counselor in the new 15th Ward Sunday School Superintendancy. I won the Oregon Geography Congress for my paper on Tonga. Edward is struggling in Florida with a cold and hard physical training.

15 May 1967, Portland

Yesterday I gave a talk in Sunday School. Dad was in San Francisco at a seminar on laboratory automation. It seems everyone was talking and dreaming about a special machine to be de-

veloped "some day"; but the machine they are talking about is the same one Dad and his colleagues have already invented. Edward seems to be better. His cold is over and he finally passed his swimming test, which consisted of jumping off a 14 foot tower into an Olympic length pool and swimming to the other end without coming up for air.

19 June 1967, Portland

Edward is an Ensign now. I performed my second baptism. Wayne is fine, as is everyone else in the family also.

6 August 1967, Portland

A friend of Sister Wood's was involved in the Church's purchase of Adam-Ondi-Ahman. The prophecies of the last days are being rapidly fulfilled: riots, mobbings, wars, earthquakes, and all sorts of trouble are more frequent. I am confident that I will live to see the Lord come in His glory.

18 August 1967, Portland

We put on our roadshow, "Pirates of the Mardi Gras" and won, naturally, so got to perform it at the five-stake show also. I played the first mate, with a cockney accent. It was great fun.

Roadshows were short plays performed by the young people, often with competition between wards and stakes. These were busy years for all of us, with church and school for me, continuing long hours at work and increasing church activity for Dad, various work assignments for Mom and Wayne, and the steady progress of life for all of us.

Dad and I went to hear Ezra Taft Benson speak (at Benson High School, appropriately, in Portland) about patriotism, the Constitution, the rule of law, and the danger of the growing threat of communism at home and abroad. Brother Benson had served as Secretary of Agriculture under President Eisenhower and at this time was a member of the Quorum of Twelve Apostles. He became President of the Church in 1985. His speech that night was very inspiring and reminded me of the precariousness of liberty in a world largely opposed to it, and of the importance of defending it.

Love of liberty and individual freedom is not simply a reflection of the American origins of the Church as some have supposed; it is an integral part of the gospel of Jesus Christ as Latter-day Saints understand it. We generally refer to it as "Free Agency".

One of the key doctrines of the restored church, as it was in the New Testament church, is that of a pre-existence. We are spirit children of a Heavenly Father and lived with Him prior to the creation of this world. In that pre-mortal world, He called us all together in a Grand Council and said that in order for us to continue to progress we needed to come into a physical world where we would learn by experience the difference between good and evil, learn to live by faith, and be tested to see if we would be obedient when not actually in His presence. In order to make it a real test, a veil of forgetfulness would be placed in our minds so we could not remember our earlier lives in heaven.

The problem was that we would make mistakes and commit sins. No unclean thing can exist in the presence of God, so it was necessary that there be a Savior who would live a perfect, sinless life and be able to take upon himself the sins of all who would repent, accept him as their Lord, obey his commandments, and try to become like him. In such a purified condition we could return to our Father. Jesus, the eldest and best among us, was chosen for that difficult assignment.

It was recognized that not all would be able keep the commandments sufficiently to return to where God lives, so additional worlds would be created, varying "degrees of glory", for those who live less virtuous lives. Paul compared these different worlds to the sun, the moon, and the stars to symbolize the various rewards given us after the final judgment; today they are called the Celestial, Terrestrial, and Telestial kingdoms. In each case, our final judgment will be to that kingdom where we can be most comfortable, most useful, and most happy.

God's proposal was called the Plan of Salvation, or Plan of Happiness, but not all were happy with the plan. Lucifer, another of our spirit brothers, objected on the grounds that some would not be saved. He proposed a plan in which everyone would be compelled to be obedient and thus would all return to heaven together. As a reward for his brilliant idea, he would assume not only the title of Savior, but the office, standing, and power of God, the Father. The problem with Lucifer's plan is that it could not work. By destroying our agency, we would not be able to learn right from wrong or experience natural consequences. We would not be able to grow and mature, but would remain forever stunted, remain forever slaves. Of course, that was his real objective.

The debates, arguments, and contention that followed are called the War in Heaven. The children of God were divided in their opinions, but most chose the Plan of Salvation, and our Father confirmed the choice of Jesus to carry it out; He cast out Lucifer and those who followed him, thus denying to them forever the privilege of living life in the mortal world and of further progression. It is written that the morning stars—the pre-existent spirits who accepted Jesus—shouted for joy!

The War in Heaven continues on earth, and it revolves around the same issue: agency, free will, freedom, and persuasion on the one hand, versus coercion, compulsion, force, and violence on the other. Once again we are asked to choose whether to follow Lucifer and the way of slavery or Jesus Christ and the Plan of Happiness. We are assured prophetically of ultimate victory, for "every knee shall bow and every tongue confess that Jesus is the Christ."

But in the meantime, things here on the ground can be difficult, especially in politics and world affairs. The 20th century was dominated by great conflicts caused by those who claim ideologically to want a utopian society and seek to force it upon the rest of us, who mainly want to be left alone, to be free. Implicitly or explicitly, all such ideologies deny God, and in practice are mechanisms for the ambitious and envious few to exercise power over others.

Joseph Smith wrote in 1839, "We have learned by sad experience that it is the nature and disposition of almost all men, as soon as they get a little authority, as they suppose, they will immediately begin to exercise unrighteous dominion." He went on to write, "No power or influence can or ought to be maintained by virtue of the priesthood, only by persuasion, by long-suffering, by gentleness and meekness, and by love unfeigned; by kindness, and pure knowledge, which shall greatly enlarge the soul without hypocrisy, and without guile. . . "

The prophet's description of the correct manner and motivation of a representative of the Lord is very clear, also the errors that can diminish priesthood power, ". . . when we undertake to cover our sins, or to gratify our pride, our vain ambition, or to exercise control or dominion or compulsion upon the souls of the children of men, in any degree of unrighteousness, behold, the heavens withdraw themselves; the Spirit of the Lord is grieved; and when it is withdrawn, Amen to the priesthood or the authority of that man."

Force, in other words, is not a part of the Lord's Plan, it belongs to the "other one".

Chapter 3

In January 1968 the communists broke a traditional period of truce and attacked over 100 cities in South Vietnam simultaneously, including the capitol of Saigon. This was the infamous Tet Offensive, the intent of which was to break the improving South Vietnamese army (ARVN), cause a general uprising in the country, and inflict heavy losses on the Americans. Despite initial confusion and dismay at the extent and intensity of the hostilities, our forces recovered quickly and fought very well. There was no uprising and the heavy losses were experienced by the North, so much so that for the only time in the war they were unable to launch a spring offensive the following year. It was a surprising military defeat for the North.

Tet was a tremendous success for them politically, however. Fighting was everywhere, even in cities that reporters and visiting politicians had come to regard as safe havens. They now found themselves in the midst of firefights rather than USO entertainers, and they were scared out of their minds. That fear translated into defeatist news reports that heartened the anti-war movement in America and also contradicted the upbeat and overly optimistic claims of President Johnson, General Westmoreland (commander of our forces in Vietnam), and the rest of the administration. Recognition of an irreparable loss of credibility contributed largely to Johnson's decision not to seek re-election.

29 January 1968, Portland

Edward and Lynn (Sparrow) will be married on 16 March

in Seattle. Grandpa Hall is staying with us while having medical tests run. It looks likely that he may stay permanently. I was recently voted "Most Intellectual" of the senior class. . . Edward is concerned about the recent Korean crisis (the north seized our ship, the "Pueblo"). I pray that things will be well with him.

The North Koreans took advantage of our involvement in nearby Vietnam to provoke us repeatedly, and each provocation risked a renewal of the war in Korea and the possibility of escalation to involve all of Asia, including the Soviets and the Chinese. Fortunately, our adversaries in Korea did not have nuclear weapons at that time or they might have been inclined to use them.

Sometime that spring a Clackamas High School alumnus who had been serving in the army came in uniform to the school and spoke about his experiences, presumably to encourage enlistment. He expressed pride in his service and country, and devotion to his unit. And yet there was a certain sadness and a hesitancy to tell details of what he had witnessed. He told how the enemy came up unexpectedly through tunnels and how difficult it was to clear them out, how dangerous it was to go through rice paddies or jungle clearings, and the lack of "front lines" to define where the battle should be. The greatest challenge was simply knowing who the enemy was. A child might walk by smiling and nodding, then throw a grenade, or a woman with child might be carrying a bomb. They did not wear uniforms.

At home, the country continued from one trauma to the next. Martin Luther King Jr. was assassinated on 4 April, followed by riots, then the assassination of President Kennedy's younger brother, Robert, on 5 June. The nation felt the need for a strong hand to lead us out of a time of confusion and violence; perhaps it was naive of us to think that could happen politically.

Dad and I attended the last Nixon rally and speech prior to the primary election. The candidate was late, which built anticipation in the crowded school auditorium where we were seated. When he finally did arrive he walked through the middle of the audience to the podium, shaking hands as he went, gave a fine speech that led to a rousing gush of patriotic fervor, and received a standing ovation. I was among those who surged around him for an autograph; he signed my pocket notebook on the page which listed Benjamin Franklin's 13 Virtues. I was delighted.

Overall, high school went well, especially my senior year, and I had a number of offers for college, including an interesting new program at Cornell that led to a Ph.D. in five years. It was tempting, but by now my heart was set on Brigham Young University in Provo, Utah. It was, after all, Dad's home town, and Don would be my roommate.

Mom and Dad took delivering me to college as a chance for a great road trip. We drove from Portland to San Diego to visit Edward and Lynn. It turned out that Edward was in training at the time, but we had a nice visit with Lynn and saw something of California in the process. From there we drove northeast through Las Vegas to St. George, Utah. We stopped at the St. George Temple early in the morning while it was still dark, just as workers were arriving. Dad and I walked over to a bench on the temple grounds and he gave me a blessing. The purpose of the priesthood is to have authority and opportunity to bless others—that first father's blessing as I was departing for college is a precious memory.

31 October 1968, Provo

I became a finalist, but did not receive a scholarship from the National Merit Scholarship Program, but did receive an Honors Scholarship from BYU, and am now in Provo studying archaeology. Last summer we put on another roadshow, "Circles of the Pettygon", a stylized version of the "Sword in the Stone." I played the main role as the wicked magician and Don played the enchanted king. Also last summer I worked in Dwyer's plywood mill, my first real job.

BYU was the largest private school west of the Mississippi. Life as a freshman in the newest dormitories, a set of high-rises called Deseret Towers, was a pleasant counterbalance to the stress of college level classes and uncertainty about majors and the future. We were, after all, still teenagers. Don and I became good friends with some of our neighbors, notably John Smurthwaite, Phil Stark, and Charley Carriker. John was a gregarious young man from La Grande, Oregon, an early center of church growth in the Northwest. He and Phil were singers, performing with the Acapella Choir, one of several excellent performing groups in the Music Department. All were intelligent, thoughtful, good students. Our late night talk sessions, sometimes over a game of *Risk*, tended to be intellectual and stimulating.

Preoccupied with studies, events on campus, and the challenge (for me) of dating, reports of the war seemed far away; the anti-war turmoil on other campuses affected us little. There were a few vigorous debates about the election, but greater enthusiasm was devoted to sports. Then too, there was the infamous "panty raid" of Deseret Towers.

Our little gang was getting ready for bed one night when we heard a commotion coming from the girls' dorms, which were set at right angles to the boys' so we could not see directly in. A large group of noisy fellows was gathered between the girls' dorms and there was hooting and chanting and calling back and forth between them and a number of the girls, who were waving their arms out their windows.

We started to go down to see what was going on, but were met by the dorm parents at the bottom of the elevators, who told us to go back to our rooms. Of course, none of the guys actually went into the girls' dorm after hours since that was against the rules, but with the noise and shouting and associated high spirits, several girls tossed panties out their windows. This was scandalous enough when word of it got around campus, but it was downright embarrassing (in more ways than one) when our rivals at the University of Utah in Salt Lake City found out about it. "Panty raid" indeed!

In declaring Archaeology as my major, I was pursuing an interest in antiquity and especially the Middle East. Perhaps that fascination was born of our family connection to the Holy Land, or perhaps of a more general interest in history. In any case, though the subject was intrinsically interesting, it was made intolerably dull by that first semester's teacher, who happened also to be the "grand old man" of the department. Social Anthropology, on the other hand, which I had second semester from Professor Merlin Myers, was fascinating not only because of the material, but also because of his excellent teaching style. He had studied at Cambridge under the great Myer Fortes. Had he acquired a subtle English accent? More importantly, he had a wonderful ability to apply principles learned among tribal society to our own experiences in life and to the gospel.

A semester of ballroom dance, along with the very social atmosphere of BYU campus life, helped me begin to overcome my fear of girls. Dating was further facilitated by organization of the student wards into "families" of about 5 or 6 boys and similar numbers of girls. Families met together once a week for Family Home Evenings and sometimes went together to church. With major social barriers overcome, it was natural eventually to go out together as couples.

25 March 1969, Provo

*Edward is in Vietnam, God save him. Since November I have been going out with a girl from our "family" in Heritage Halls (*a nearby girls' dorm*). She is a Russian major—her name in Russian is Darya.*

Edward's squadron was assigned to the *USS Enterprise*, the first nuclear powered aircraft carrier, named for the famous World War II carrier. It was the longest naval vessel in the world and had a crew of 4,600. As is true of military experience generally, much of Edward's time was spent in training.

On 14 January 1969, after an overhaul in Hawaii and while engaging in a final drill prior to proceeding to Vietnam, a rocket on a parked F-4 overheated and exploded, setting off a series of additional explosions and fires. The flight deck was full and each fighter-bomber was loaded with eight 5-inch rockets and six 500 pound bombs. Each aircraft also held nine tons of fuel. Eight of the rockets went off in the first 20 seconds, but then things got worse as fuel ignited and bombs exploded. Rockets penetrated four decks down; one destroyed the room Edward had been in only minutes before. In the end, 27 personnel were killed, 314 were injured, and 15 aircraft were destroyed; no enemy was ever able to damage the *Enterprise* as badly as that accident. The ship went back to Pearl Harbor for repairs, finally heading back to the Gulf of Tonkin on 1 March 1969.

World events further delayed their arrival. On 14 April the North Koreans shot down one of our reconnaissance aircraft over the East Japan Sea, killing all 31 crewmen. Relations on the Korean peninsula, always tense, had been particularly difficult since they seized the *USS Pueblo* the previous year, falsely claiming it had strayed into their waters. The *Enterprise* was deployed there along with three other aircraft carriers and their accompanying cruisers and destroyers. It was the largest force sent to Korea since the Korean War.

Hostile forces not only observe each other, they probe and test defenses and response times, so it is common for there to be small encounters, always with the risk that events can get out of hand. News reports at the time told how two Russian Migs approached the carrier force and the *Enterprise* sent up two F-4s to intercept them. Our aircraft chased them almost to Russian airspace before breaking off the pursuit. It was only much later that we learned Edward was in the backseat of one of them.

The summer of 1969 while awaiting my mission call I worked again at Dwyer's plywood mill in Lent's. It was good, hard work, and paid relatively well for the time. Missionaries are expected to support themselves as much as possible, which meant saving up prior to the call. In my case that amounted to a little more than $800, which was not nearly enough. Mom and Dad very kindly agreed to make up the difference. Looking back now, and especially in light of later events, I realize more keenly what a great sacrifice it was for them.

By any standard, the summer of 1969 was filled with historic events. On 21 July Neil Armstrong became the first man to walk on the moon, accompanied soon thereafter by Buzz Aldrin. We watched the event live on television along with the rest of the world. Grandpa Hall did not fully understand what was going on. Mom spoke loudly to overcome his hearing loss, "Those men are on the moon, Pop." He grunted. "Huh. You don't say." Then silence for a moment. "What are those big suits they are wearing?" "Those are spacesuits," she answered. "They need to wear them because there isn't any air on the moon." Another silence. "Huh. Why would anybody want to go to a place like that?" He was tired of the show, got up, and went to his room.

The news from outer space was probably most exciting to those portions of the younger generation who had grown up on *Star Trek* and who were scientifically inclined. There was also a contingent of youth who preferred more earthy excitements. For these, the concert and "fair" at Woodstock, New York, became the defining experience of the sixties, filled with drugs, rock music, and sex. The rest of us thought rutting about in a muddy field all weekend was so far beneath civilized life that it belonged on another planet.

*****

Our group of priests loved to speculate about where we might be sent for our missions. It was idle speculation, of course, because we could not predict it and everyone knew of young men who were fluent in Spanish being sent to Mississippi or who studied French in school but were sent to Mexico. Genealogy could be suggestive and it was not uncommon for someone to be sent to where his immigrant ancestors had come from, but there were lots of exceptions to that rule as well. In the end we would go wherever the Lord wanted us.

From time to time returned missionaries would give talks about their missions, sometimes in a setting where they could show slides, and we would become excited about our prospects. Over the course of a few months, two elders came back from Austria and showed wonderful pictures of beautiful mountains, lush woodlands, and rolling fields, with quaint villages and cities filled with all sorts of interesting buildings and friendly people. We agreed that Austria would be the best place to serve.

Calls began to come in—Don to North Germany, Phil Stark and John Smurthwaite both to Italy, others to various locations around the world. My application inexplicably sat on Bishop Waddell's desk. It was forgotten, then needed other details, then was delayed between Bishop and Stake President, then took longer than expected at church headquarters. Finally the letter arrived in early August. I happened to walk down to the mailbox with Mom that day and she did not want me to wait for Dad, so I opened it while walking back up the gravel road to home:

5 August 1969, Salt Lake City, Utah

Dear Elder Saxey:

You are hereby called to be a missionary of The Church of Jesus Christ of Latter-day Saints and to labor in the Austrian Mission. You are scheduled to enter the Mission Home in Salt Lake City at 119 North Main Street on Saturday, September 27, 1969.

Your presiding officers have recommended you as one worthy to represent the Church of our Lord as a Minister of the Gospel. It will be your duty to live righteously, to keep the commandments of the Lord, to honor the holy Priesthood which you bear, to increase your testimony of the divinity of the Restored Gospel of Jesus Christ, to be an exemplar in your life of all the Christian virtues, and so to conduct yourself as a devoted servant of the Lord that you may be an effective advocate and messenger of the Truth. We repose in you our confidence and extend to you our prayers that the Lord will help you thus to meet your responsibilities.

The Lord will reward the goodness of your life, and greater blessings and more happiness than you have yet experienced await you as you serve Him humbly and prayerfully in this labor of love among His children. . . .

Sincerely yours,
David O. McKay, President

Along with the call letter was a packet of instructions concerning travel, passport, vaccinations, the mission, finances, and other logistics. Another letter followed soon thereafter:

18 August 1969, Vienna, Austria

Dear Elder Saxey:

Welcome to the Austrian Mission! You have been called to serve in one of the most wonderful mission fields of the Church. We are enclosing some historical sketches that will help you to become better acquainted with the country and with the people among whom you will proselyte the next two years. . . . Inasmuch as nearly all your proselyting will be done in German, it will hardly be necessary to bring the Standard Works in English. . . .

Some of the information on the sheet passed on to you about the Austrian Mission is out of date. The average monthly cost of our mission is 100 dollars. We are asking each elder to bring along white trousers, a tie, and belt that he will need in performing baptisms. Do not bring along loud sport jackets, vests, socks, etc. In warm weather we do not require that our missionaries wear hats. In cold weather we recommend that a warm Russian-type hat be purchased over here. Austrian suits hold up much better than do American ones.

The Lord bless you to the end that your mission may become an unforgettable, spiritual and intellectual experience.

Sincerely your brother,
Charles W. Broberg, Mission President

It turned out that the group of missionaries sent to Austria that Fall was the largest ever to go at one time. If my application had arrived in Salt Lake City earlier in the Summer I probably would have been called elsewhere according to the needs of the work, but the Lord knows where and when to send His servants. He considers the desires of their hearts and extends kindness to them—and He had just given me a most wonderful blessing. I could not have been more thrilled.

Now came the scramble to get ready: new suit, new shoes, shots at the county clinic. Dad gave me a camera to take with me to Austria, an Argus C3. He had meant for it to be his own old Argus that he had used during World War II, but, discovering that his was not repairable, he searched the camera shops for another. It was a great little, light-weight, reliable 35 mm. The main drawback was that I did not use it enough.

My farewell Sacrament Meeting was held 14 September 1969 with Clair Cantwell conducting, Sister Geneal Wood as chorister, and Sister Maxine Hill as organist. The youth speakers were Laurie Howard and Scott Taylor. There were two musical numbers by Maxine Hill and Melvin Randall. I spoke, Dad spoke, President Don Wood spoke, and Bishop Clyde Waddell was the concluding speaker. As I looked around at these good souls and heard their kind words, my heart was filled with love and gratitude to them and to the Lord for placing me among such faithful Saints.

President Wood compared my successful mission to the opening, sacrament, and closing hymns we sang: *How Firm a Foundation* was the preparation I had been given; *I Need Thee Every Hour* was the great dependence of every missionary on the continued guidance of the Spirit; and *The Spirit of God Like a Fire is Burning* was the success that would result as I followed that guidance. There was a short reception afterwards with refreshments. Otto Bluemel, who had taught two of my four years of high school German, though not a member, was there and was very encouraging.

The next day at work, Mom asked Bishop Waddell if it would be possible for me to baptize her before I left for Utah the following week. Bishop, of course, said it was. She also asked that he not tell anyone because she did not want people to make a fuss over her. He said he would not, except he would have to tell the Relief Society President, who at that time was Marilyn Ward.

A day or so later the Bishop called me to ask that I come to the Stake Center on Saturday to perform a baptism. I thought nothing of it since our leaders often gave opportunity to priests and new elders to perform ordinances whenever possible. Unknown to me, similar calls to attend the Stake baptismal service went out to Dad and Wayne, without explanations why.

Prior to the service was a prayer meeting. I waited in a small room with a number of others while candidates for baptism and other priesthood bearers entered; then my Dear Mother entered, all dressed in white, and sat down beside me. She asked if I was surprised; I said I knew she would join when she was ready. After the prayer and instructions, we filed into the larger font room. The room was packed, with some standing in the back. Dad was seated just behind where Mom and I were to sit. The congregation was singing *I Stand All Amazed* as we walked in; Dad's eyes grew large, there was a puzzled expression on his face, and he stopped singing. He was all amazed indeed!

After the baptism, dried and dressed in our Sunday clothes, we went to an adjacent classroom to perform the laying on of hands for confirmation of membership and bestowal of the Gift of the Holy Ghost. So many brethren were present and wanted to participate that we had difficulty fitting together in the circle—Dad, President Wood, Bishop Waddell, Brother Cantwell, Brother Hill, Brother Ward, and many others. The Spirit was very strong, and, as is usually the case, specifics of the blessing are not well recalled, but I do remember blessing her in genealogical work and performing vicarious work for the dead in the temple. She and Dad subsequently became temple workers and served many years in the Portland Temple.

At the conclusion of the meeting Mom took Bishop Waddell aside and said, "I told you not to tell everyone." He replied, "I didn't. Only Sister Ward, like I said." But of course, that was all that was needed. Mom and Dad were well known in the ward and stake, and much loved. Grandpa Hall was not pleased, though, and a few weeks later made arrangements to live with Hal and his family in Mexico City. Apparently Catholicism was preferable to Mormonism after all.

A few days later I took my first airplane flight, a flight from Portland to Salt Lake City, a flight into a new life. I did not know that by the time I returned the world I had known and loved would be changed forever.

Chapter 4

28 September 1969, Salt Lake City

Today is my second day in the Mission Home at Salt Lake City. We heard Richard L. Evans speak about the temple endowment, which we shall receive tomorrow. . . Last week I had the pleasure of baptizing and confirming Mother . . . It was the greatest day of my life.

In the temple individuals are prepared for life in eternity. The major ordinance is called The Endowment, in which the creation is dramatized; our relationships to God, to our first parents, and to Christ are illustrated; and the participants formally covenant to obey God's commandments. Other temple ordinances include baptisms on behalf of dead ancestors and sealing of families together for time and all eternity.

29 September 1969, Salt Lake City

Today I received the temple endowment and begin to perceive the wisdom of God in giving it to us. Eternity and the works of eternity take on greater significance after the endowment. . . Edward returned safely from his first tour of duty in Vietnam aboard the USS Enterprise. Dad was called as Sunday School Superintendant.

30 September 1969, Salt Lake City

Today Elder Franklin D. Richards (an Assistant to the

Quorum of the Twelve Apostles) set me apart as a missionary in the Church. The records will say it took place tomorrow, but our schedule had to be rearranged because of the coming conference. It is rough trying to memorize the discussions and accomplish all the things we have to do, learn all we must learn, and be to all the meetings we must attend.

I did not know it at the time, but Elder Richards had been the Northwestern States Mission President prior to President Wood's tenure. When I met him he was in a small office in the old Church Office Building, had white hair, and seemed a little distracted, probably because of preparations for the semiannual church conference which was coming up that weekend.

In those years, all newly called missionaries had about a week of training at the Mission Home in Salt Lake City across from the Temple; most had not been through the temple prior to our calls; and we were usually set apart by General Authorities (to be set apart is to be formally blessed with the authority and responsibility of a calling by the laying on of hands, receiving also any additional blessings the Spirit might inspire).

From there, missionaries to English speaking assignments went directly to their missions while the rest of us went to Language Training Missions (LTM) on or near the BYU campus in Provo for two months prior to going out. The German LTM was in Amanda Knight Hall, a beautiful old former dormitory built in English Tudor style. Missionaries are organized into companionships of two individuals, districts of about three to six companionships, and zones of several districts. The German LTM was one zone; the Italian LTM was nearby.

1 October 1969, Provo

Today we arrived at the Language Training Mission at Provo, Utah. My companion is Elder Wilde, a really terrific fellow from Los Angeles; our district is called Feldkirch. We sure don't have much time free here. I am somewhat concerned about chance encounters with Darya when we go on campus. I saw John Smurthwaite and Don Waddell again here at the LTM . . .

3 October 1969, Provo

Well, here I am with a free two hours and accomplishing nothing. Elder Wilde is a great guy, but we are not the same sort of person. I would prefer to be up on campus getting books, seeing things (maybe people), and having fun. But instead I am stuck here in the old Women's Gymnasium, watching him play basketball (I have no outfit). I know the LTM is of the Lord and yet . . . At times I have felt a great peace and joy in this work. But at other times I feel lost, like a ship without a rudder. . .

John Smurthwaite introduced me last year to the writings of J.R.R. Tolkien, namely The Hobbit *and* The Trilogy of the Rings. *I have not been the same since. Fantasy novels drawing on the ancient legends and myths of England, Ireland, Scandinavia, and Germany, they are delightful things. I shall be always grateful to John for them. They touch thoughts and feelings which are very deep in the soul—the goodness of life and nature, the eternal conflict of good and evil, the saga of the quest. These books have renewed my ancient love of folklore, the Teutonic myths in particular, as well as my love of nature. I miss Darya.*

10 October 1969, Provo

Liebe Eltern,

. . . That first week or so, as I hadn't received any letter, was really rough. I felt detached from the world—cast adrift, so to speak. Besides, I had a cold. But now everything is looking better. They reorganized our districts according to our language ability and experience. I am now in Bremen District and have a new companion, Elder Labrum. . . .

At 7:15 we have district Mtg (actually only prayer); at 7:30 Zone Mtg (all the German speaking missionaries); at 8:00 class 'til 10, when we have an hour of study ("retention"), followed by another hour of class; at 5:00 a free hour; at 6:00 dinner; at 7:00 retention 'til 10. On Fri we have proselyting class. On Sat we have class from 9-11, and Culture Class from 11-12, and then a free day.

As you may gather, it's a busy day. Standing in line for meals we study. During evening retention we have one hour of talking to a native speaker . . . The other night we talked to a Sis. from Heidelberg. She really has a great testimony, being a convert of 8 wks. It was most inspiring.

Love,
Rod

While we were at the LTM the Church relaxed the rule on missionaries' hours—instead of arising at 6:00 am, we had the option of arising as late as 6:30. That extra half hour made life a great deal easier for many of us. There was enough that we had to learn and adjust to without being tired as well. Bedtime was still 10:30.

Brother Labrum proved to be a pleasant companion, faithful, cheery, and encouraging. His German was very good also, so we were soon able to "live our language" nearly continuously. The constant use of our new language quickly crept into our journals and letters, which suffered because of German constructions working their way into our English prose. Everyday speech was even worse.

English speaking missionaries are usually addressed by the title, *Elder*, which seems a little odd at first since they are so young. The German equivalent is *Ältester*, which actually means "eldest." This is too much of an incongruity, so they are simply called "Brother", *Bruder*, like other members. There were sister missionaries as well, but very few, and they did not have a translation problem, being called "Sister", *Schwester*.

12 October 1969, Provo

Liebe Eltern,

Thanks for sending Edward and Lynn's letter. . . I hope Grampa's O.K. . . .

I was appointed to represent our district in the "Live Your Language Committee." . . .

We all went to the BYU-New Mexico game the other night. It was really good—we won . . . *Wunderbar*! The *Deutsch* is coming amazingly easily. This evening I give a District Home Family Evening lesson—*auf Englisch, aber*.

As I sit here, I recall the importance of the temple instruction. . . The instruction there, the knowledge, is indescribably ancient and yet as fresh as morning—and as vital as life's day. It may seem strange, but it isn't really—not when viewed from its proper perspective. You'll see what I mean. . . .

It snowed here the other day (this morning, in fact). The mts. are really beautiful. . . .

Love, Rod

18 October 1969, Provo

. . . It is Mission Conference and for our evening meeting the 3Ds entertained. The first half of the program was excellent— songs of love and life. The second half of it, however, was extraordinary. They sang and spoke of the restoration and the westward movement. After this, their testimonies were born with power and conviction. Then they sang "Come, Come, Ye Saints".

Rarely have I felt the Spirit of Truth so strongly. One spoke of the power of a smile to conversion; another of the "jet-accelerated take-off" we receive at the LTM; the third of many important spiritual things, the most significant of which to me was his mention of the verity of the Eternal War in which we are presently engaged, and in which we missionaries constitute the front-line troops. Constantly repeated in the total presentation was the reference to the Camp of Israel, antiquity, and other ancient and meaningful things. May I always remember the eternal, continuous, and significant nature of our struggle against the great darkness. They recommended the reading of Ezekial 2 and Ephesians 4:2, in that order.

19 October 1969, Provo

Today the Bremen District fasted and held our own testimony meeting. The Spirit was manifest in abundance. It was one of those rare occasions when eight 19 year-old boys allowed them-

selves to each shed a few tears in the presence of peers. That their names may not be lost in memory, I shall now record them: Brüder Kent Duke, Bruce Hirst, Jeff Labrum, Welker, Olsen, Parry, and Patten. They are terrific fellows. I feel my testimony has really grown because of them. Their strength is amazing. I had at first doubts about Olsen and Welker, but now I know they know and that they are really great. I feel a special kinship of spirit with Bruder Duke, like unto the one I feel for John Smurthwaite. I love each of these brethren greatly.

In our district testimony meeting we spoke of our impressions of each other; Br. Welker drew my name. He was an intense young man with blond hair and tightly controlled emotion, not to mention excellent German. He bore his testimony in German, saying of me that his first impression was, "*ein kalter Stein*", a cold stone. He then said huskily that he had come to know that I had great love for each of them, more love than any of them, which was an exaggeration, but kind of him to say. I still pondered the problem, why did I come across as cold?

Ein kalter Stein? How could I change that?

25 *Oktober* 1969, Provo

Liebe Eltern,

. . . We started second level German (memorization of the dialogues). It's rougher, no doubt about it. Most of the day we stand in class repeating the sentences after the teacher. It's a lot to learn—and every ending, every letter, has to be perfect. (In 2 days we've learned 7 pages.) Our district has been doing great about Living Our Language. It's really not hard now . . . it's exciting to see people pick this stuff up.

We've only been able to have Culture Class twice, but it's been great. German history so far is right down my line of interest. . . . (I think I might turn my college studies toward) Teutonic language study with emphasis on History and Folklore. This is pretty much what it was at the end of last year in Anthropology, but the feeling is now (stronger).

It sounds like things are going great at home, what with preparations for Christmas and everything. Say, Dad, I made an impression on our *Zuhörer* the other night (the district talks in free discussion with a *Zuhörer*, or native speaker). She asked me to order a meal and for dessert I asked for *Lebkuchen*—which started a 10 minute discussion on the nature and merits of said item. . . .

The other day we ran into Charlie Carriker, another member of our little gang at Deseret Towers. He's really a great fellow, and has decided he wants to go on a mission. His father objects, though. It's too bad. Things like that make me really appreciate you all, and all the things you've done for me.

I managed to see John S. the other day too. . . . He was sort of depressed, so we talked quite a while. It's slower for the Italians because none of them has studied the language before, so they have to really start at the beginning. One fellow that's quite a bit like John is Elder Duke. He, however, doesn't appear to get depressed like John and I sometimes do. . . .

Well, I better get busy. I have to give a talk *auf Deutsch* on Thurs. (Say, I sure am glad to have the recorder flute. I only use it for a few minutes every once in awhile, but it helps relax.) . . .

Servös (Austrian *adieu*), Rod

29 Oct 1969, Portland

Dear Rod,

. . . Bishop Waddell read part of your letter to the ward leaders this last Sunday. Your extremely fine wording and thought brought tears to Clyde's eyes. He had difficulty continuing—he did so appreciate your letter. We are all so proud of you. Your Mother does not even drink coffee now.

The tree replanting is going well—over 50 so far. Mirkwood will look better in a couple of years. Hobbiton will be in the corner where we talked of putting the waterfall. A round Hobbit House with a round door and a fireplace—could be a sauna with the door closed. Whole place about 8 feet in diameter. Oh, yes, I finished the books long ago.

Love, Dad

Over the years the trees grew thick and tall all around Mom and Dad's place in Portland. The Hobbit House was made of ferrocement, set into a corner of the hillside, and had a large open barbecue in back; the chimney stuck up through the ivy that Dad planted on the hill slope and that eventually covered everything except the door. Our first Christmas tree in Portland was a living fir and was planted directly in front of the house about fifty feet from the front door. It grew as a tall, symmetrical cone, like a wizard's hat, so we named it Gandalf.

3 November 1969, Provo

Today I passed off the First Discussion—no sweat. Tonight our Freie Rede Lehrerin, *Schwester Boden, a wonderful woman, told us about door approaches and for the first time I think I see what I must do: pray to be led by the Spirit.*

The *Uniform System System for Teaching Investigators* was a set of lessons in discussion format that was created as a means of bringing more consistency to the missionary work. We memorized it word for word, including the ideal, hoped for responses of the archetypal investigator, Brother Brown, or in our case, *Bruder Braun*. It was based on *The Anderson Plan*, lessons developed by Richard Lloyd Anderson as a missionary in the Northwestern States Mission from 1946-49, and grew out of a pooling of experience by mission presidents, including important early applications of the program in the Northwestern States Mission under President Richards and President Wood. The lessons I had received as an 11 year old were part of that lesson plan. Elder Anderson, incidentally, after training in Greek and Classics, went on to become a professor of Church History and Doctrine. One of my favorite classes at BYU was his Honors course on The New Testament. Professor Anderson was always perceptive and insightful; he had an oval face, silvery hair, and the reasoned smile of a classicist. I sat front row center.

6 November 1969, Provo

This morning started with a beautiful sunrise, and I had a great feeling all day. Shortly before lunch Bruder Bennion, the Mission President, called me to be the new Zone Leader, whom we affectionately refer to as Der Grosse Käse *("The Big Cheese"). Bruder Hirst will be my counselor and Bruder Labrum will be the new District Leader. Bruder Duke said that Bruder Anderson last night had a dream in which Bruder Hirst had that calling as Number 2. He didn't say whether he saw me as ZL.*

13 November 1969, Houston

Dear "Elder Rod",

. . . This experience you are about to enjoy will set the stage in spirituality for your entire life. Stay close to the Lord. Be very prayerful and make the code of your mission "to be teachable". As you do these things I know great success and happiness will be yours. I have heard that your wonderful mission has found new life and the Elders are enjoying success like never before—sounds tremendous!!

I'm happy to report the Wood's have a couple of baptisms coming up. Monday we baptize a nurse from Providence and on Dec 6 a young physical therapist and her family will be baptized. She is so golden it is unbelievable. She gave "book answers" last Monday for the 1st discussion and then offered a great and simple prayer. Both will make tremendous converts from the Catholic Church.

Please forgive the "jumpy" handwriting. I'm on a plane headed for Houston where I will give a paper tomorrow on a new anti-tumor agent we have been experimenting with. It has excellent prospects against some types of cancer. . . Our prayers are always with you.

Pres. Wood

On 15 November 1969 anti-war demonstrators held the largest anti-war demonstration in U.S. history, attracting some

250,000 participants to a march on Washington, D.C. We were un-
aware of it.

15 November 1969, Provo

Dear Mom & Dad,

. . . Things here are fine and today is especially good. I
passed off the third discussion today (gave it to the teacher with a
minimum of errors); did chores; and, I think, rectified a problem in
the Zone. . . .

Last week I conducted my first Sunday School Opening
Exercises. It was exciting, if not very well done. Br Hirst and I will
trade off conducting Sunday School and Priesthood Mtgs. One of
the other things I have to do is give out all assignments in the
Zone. That means trying to help 108 missionaries develop the potential in them. . . And, of course, it's all or nearly all, in German.

Bruder Labrum is really a great fellow, quite tolerant of my
idiosyncrasies. He also comes up with some good ideas to help the
Zone. . . Yes, I saw Don before he left. After all, we're in the same
bldg. He came around during retention and said see you later. We'll
probably see each other in Europe. . .

I have a phone in my room as Zone Leader, for business
only, of course. I presume they will let us call home for Thanksgiving (and that can count for 'bye on the 2nd). . . . I'll have to check
things out with Br. Bennion, the Zone Counselor.

Boy, the sunrises & sunsets around here have been terrific
lately, with all sorts of tonations and contrasts. I would try to take a
picture of them, but it wouldn't come out.

Well, between this paragraph and the last we've had a major problem—a lost missionary. We spent 45 mins. searching for him only to find out he was sitting in the car out front—two rules down the drain (no being in cars & no excessive visiting with parents or friends). I guess it's time to refresh people's memories of the rules and why we have them.

. . . (The) work load is probably the heaviest of any school, and every minute is terrific.

I love you and hope everyone is O.K. Rod

29 November 1969, Provo

Time is passing so quickly. I have had many very spiritual experiences. I periodically have to speak to the members of the Zone and sometimes admonish them, and I know the Spirit of Lord is usually with me. I felt the Spirit testify strongly recently while reading "Christ and the Inner Life" by Truman Madsen. I know the Christ lives and that He died for us. This is a wonderful thing to know.

29 November 1969, Portland

Dear Elder Saxey:

. . . We want you to know that we think about you often and that we pray for you as you are away from home, doing your duty and giving of your service. And that we are proud of you as you represent this Stake of the Church, your family, and your brothers and sisters in the gospel. . . .

Portland Stake Presidency
Thomas Emmett, Grant K. Remington, Reed R. Madsen

Someone in the government decided that our increased need for soldiers in Vietnam should be met by a lottery, thus making it more difficult for those in higher socioeconomic classes to avoid service. Birthdates in 1950 were drawn by lot on 1 December 1969 and those who were born on those dates were drafted in the order drawn. We all listened to a voice on the radio calling out the dates and assigning them numbers in sequence: some groaned, some cheered, all knew this was an important predictor of our futures. For the next two years we all had 4-D deferrals as religious ministers, but when we returned we would, if fit, be 1-A and eligible for the draft. The expectation at the time was that only the first couple dozen would have to go, but in the end draftees extended to number 195; my number was 250. I felt relieved not so much about not having to go, but that I was free to choose whether and when and in which branch of the service.

1 December 1969, Portland

Dearest Rod,

Well, by now I'll bet you are really excited—I'm with you in spirit. . . .

Edward and Lynn called last night. . . . Edward is not able to leave the squadron and will be back in Vietnam for a nine month tour, April thru December. It makes me sick. We will all unite in prayer. It's the only way. Jan and Feb he'll be in the Caribbean Sea and March he'll be home. Apr is the fateful month—they go down around the cape and then to the same base he was in before, only on the *America* this time. . . .

Love You Dear, Mom

The departing missionaries made idle talk as we waited in the pre-dawn chill for the bus that would take us to the airport. Several of us decided that this was a great adventure like the Hobbit books and we identified with the characters. Brother Duke was Frodo and I was Sam.

Chapter 5

3 December 1969, Vienna

> *Now I am in Vienna. After a four hour wait we flew out of Salt Lake Airport yesterday morning at 8 am and arrived here at one in the afternoon local time. We had stops in Denver, New York, and Brussels. In Brussels I bought a postcard—in French! Travel companions were Brothers Nielson, R, Wilde, Wilkinson, and Ogilvie. Tomorrow I travel by train to Linz, then on to Wels, a little town in Upper Austria. My companion will be Bruder Archibald in Urfahr District. It is beautiful outside; the season's first snow started to fall as we arrived.*

President Charles W. Broberg and his Assistants met us at the airport and drove us to the Mission Home, a formidable grey building with gables. I was delighted with the architecture—all around were other wonderful buildings with ornamental touches from various eras, mostly the nineteenth century in the neighborhood of the Home. The president proved loquacious and cheery, a very positive and enthusiastic man, with much more energy than expected for his age, which I guessed correctly to be over 65. He had a perceptive wit which at times grew into a wry sense of humor, remarking on the Mission Home steps about our arriving with the falling snow. By morning the snow was thick; we had come to the land of Christmas.

4 December 1969, Vienna

Brother and Sister Edward Saxey:

This is just a short note to let you know how thankful and happy we are that your son has arrived safely and in excellent health and spirits in the great country of Austria. He has already embarked upon his duties as a Missionary in the very interesting city of Wels. His companion is Elder John Archibald, who has been selected for this very highly regarded privilege of introducing a new Missionary into the work of our Heavenly Father, because of his ability, knowledge of the Gospel, faithfulness, and understanding of the problems that now and then confront Elders who must learn a foreign language, proselyting methods, as well as some rather strange customs all at the same time.

We appreciate most sincerely the support and encouragement you have given your son over the years that have made it possible for him to accept the call to serve here in this beautiful land. He will be a tremendous asset to us in teaching the Gospel to these fine Austrian people. Your continued love, faith, and prayers will have a great influence on his success and happiness, and we encourage you to write frequent, cheerful, and encouraging letters to him. . . .

Please accept again our sincere thanks for sending your fine son to us and for the service you render the Church as you support him here. May the Lord pour out his choicest blessings upon you, and be assured of our great interest in assisting your son to achieve success and happiness as he serves as a humble servant of the Master.

Faithfully your brother
Charles W. Broberg, Mission President

5 *Dezember* 1969, Wels

Dear Mom & Dad,

Well, we made it so far. I am now in Wels, a little town of about 40,000 near Linz. . . . Fridays are our diversion day—letter writing, bath, and today at least, shopping. I haven't seen much of the city yet, so I can't describe anything on that account, except that it is bloody cold, with about 4 inches of snow.

We live at Eiselsbergstrasse 22, 4600 Wels, Austria. Our landlady is a really nice little old lady, who, by the way, is a member of the Church. We are probably the only missionaries in Austria renting from a member . . . We have no central heating—only a coal stove in the kitchen. We sleep in *Federbetten*, big tics filled with down, no blankets!

After arriving in *Wien* and going through customs, President Broberg and several missionaries greeted us and took us to the mission home. That night was spent in a hotel nearby. The next day we had an orientation, a great lunch by their Hungarian cook (a cauliflower soup that was out of this world), and took the 2:00 pm train to Wels, the Transalpine. On the train Br. Duke and I sat by two fellows from Turkey. Communication was difficult because they did not speak English or German, but they apparently are wanderers—they worked in *Wien* at a textile factory, are now heading for Brussels, eventually wanting to end up in the U.S.

Br. Fagar, also going to Wels, and I arrived here at 4:20 (it was supposed to be 4:05, but Austrian trains are notoriously late) and were promptly greeted by Br. Archibald. We then waited 3 hrs for Br. Mauchley to arrive. This is the first time in a long while that two pairs of elders are here. . . . After we found our way to our respective apartments we went to a local *Gasthaus* for dinner, roast pork with onions for me; it was terrific.

Later, as I was unpacking, our *Hausfrau* (landlady), Schwester Reisenbichler, came in to introduce herself and to present me with a plate of nuts & fruit & candy & cookies from a Christmas pixie (a little devil called the *Krampus*—Dec is full of days where things like this are done, holidays nearly the whole month). That was really nice of her. . . .

We couldn't see much on the flight over—Kansas really is flat and dull, we saw lights over New York, and Europe was cloudy everywhere. One thing about the flight—they fed us too much; every time we turned around it was mealtime. We stopped in Brussels; I hope you get the postcard I sent. All that French, 'couldn't understand a word.

My companion is a great fellow. He has a sense of humor like the Cantwells, is from Idaho, and has been in Austria about a year and in Wels three months. . . . I love you.

Auf wiedersehen, Rod

10 December 1969, Portland

Dearest Rod,

Enclosed is one of our front page headlines:

SNOW BURIES EASTERN EUROPE

Vienna

The appearance of Soviet soldiers on the frontier between Communist Hungary and neutral Austria Tuesday did not signal a sudden East-West crisis.

The Russians were brought within sight of Austrian border sentries by a snow calamity the like of which the area has not experienced for many years.

Soviet and Hungarian troops were digging out trucks and autos, but failed in their efforts to keep the international Vienna-Budapest Highway open. The important artery, like many other roads and rail connections in Central and Eastern Europe, remained blocked for many miles by snowdrifts up to 6 feet high.

Catastrophe Reported

The Austrian press and radio spoke of a "snow catastrophe," and the information media of adjacent Communist countries also tended to dramatize the weather emergency.

State authorities seized on the winter vagaries of nature to explain why Prague housewives could not find any meat at their butchers, why Budapest food markets were without vegetables, and why coal was scarce in many snow bound cities.

Shortages of basic supplies, in part caused by a rundown transportation system, had been felt in Poland, Czechoslovakia and Hungary before winter set in with harsh suddenness last week. The massive snowfalls over the weekend have greatly increased such economic difficulties.

. . . Mom

12 December 1969, Wels

. . . Two other missionaries are in the other side of town—Mauchley and Fagar. We make a great group. We have had many doors slammed in our faces already. It seems that everyone has

been approached this way, door to door, and either know "every-thing" or have no interest. We did contact three ladies the other night who seem pretty golden—we were invited back and it looks hopeful.

One little sister really impresses me—Schwester Kapp. She has had such a rough life. Her children left her, her husband is dead, she was a prisoner during the war and was badly mistreated. She now lives in a tiny one room attic apartment with no water—we bring it up to her in buckets. Through it all though, she retains a good heart, more than most people have.

There are still plenty of golden people left here, but all around are signs of a decadent society. . . . The last baptism in Wels was two years ago.

12 *Dezember* 1969, Wels

Dear Mom & Dad,

Well, I've been here more than a week and am learning all sorts of things, like riding a bike, saddle sores and all. It still scares the daylights out of me, but it's coming. The bike only cost about $52, which isn't too bad. I had to buy a lot of things here at the start, but the prices are great, so money will be no problem; in fact, I should be able to get by usually on about $100 rather than $120. Rent is $13/mo.; my new suit cost $52 (a really great one with vest); an Austrian heavy overcoat $32; a Russian hat about $13. A day's meals usually run about $3.

On Wednesday we go over to Linz (15-30 minutes by train) for District Mtg. This last Tuesday, though, the District Leader wanted to come over and work with Br. Archibald for a day, so I went to his companion for overnight. He was sick, so we didn't do any proselyting, just visited some members. It was kind of neat, riding around on the *Strassenbahn* (streetcar); and besides, they have hot running water—wow! And their room is warm at night—central heating—double wow! The next day after the meeting we returned to Wels. That evening Br. A and I followed up a referral and taught three ladies the first part of the First Discussion and were invited back again—that's really something for Wels. In any case, we've got to get this place moving. No baptisms for two years here.

The hard part is just getting in to talk with people. That's the trouble with tracting door to door: too many slams before the message is delivered. We introduce ourselves and—"*Ach, ja. Mormonen!*" Slam! That gets old fast. Of course, this is a hard area. *Wien*, Graz, Salzburg, it's moving faster there. . .

The other day we had dinner—the noon meal—with a member family. Boy, was that good! A thick potato-vegetable soup, a huge portion of apple strudel, and johannisbeer juice afterwards. It was really terrific. I am not quite used to waiting until after the meal to drink anything. The pastries are great. I think I might eat too much here. . . .

Love, Rod

One of my greatest challenges that first week was learning to ride a bike—life on the farm and near hilly Happy Valley had not leant itself to bike riding. Br. Archibald was very patient and tried hard not to laugh as I wobbled my way around in circles in the parking lot the first time. Perhaps it would have been not quite so difficult if there were not a layer of ice with overlying inches of snow to contend with; every few feet the wheels would slip out from under me and I would land in a heap on the ice. Fortunately, the overcoat and multiple layers of clothing provided some cushioning.

Despite the parking lot practice, my first trip downtown resulted in a slow speed crash into the bumper of a car parked in front of the restaurant. Apparently my practice had not included sufficient time with the brakes. There was no damage, but the owner of the car came out and said something very loudly, accompanied with gestures. That particular vocabulary had not been covered in our studies. No doubt it was dialect.

Another practice that was new for a boy accustomed to showering every night before bed was only being able to take a bath once a week. We did not have time to go through the laborious process of heating water for a bath at our apartment, so on our preparation days went to the *Stadtbad* (the municipal bathhouse). This proved a high point of the week, with all the hot steamy water we wanted in clean showers with ample elbow room. In between times we became adept at the use of the sink and a washcloth.

Wels is a pleasant small city in Upper Austria (*Oberösterreich*), a local market center since Roman times. The town square is shaped like an elongated sausage with a medieval tower-gate at one end and a beautiful church with a *Zwiebelturm* ("onion tower", referring to the shape of its steeple) at the other. As in other Austrian towns, most buildings are painted in gentle pastel shades and most oldtown streets are cobblestone, which makes bike riding a jarring, at times teeth-rattling experience. The surrounding countryside is nearly flat with a few rolling hills. Wels boasts a small castle where the Emperor, Maximilian I, liked to resort and where he died in 1519. *Linz an der Donau* is the nearest large city.

15 *Dezember* 1969, *Wien*

Dear Br. Saxey!

Just writing to wish you a Merry Christmas and a happy new year. I just can't believe how large this city of *Wien* is. My companion and I are having quite a bit of success. He had a baptism the first Sunday after we arrived (the 7th). We also plan on having a baptism this week. The people here in the branch are wonderful. I know that with the Lord's help, we'll be able to make the work here in Austria go forth faster than ever before. I want you to know how much I appreciate you and I think of you often.

Bis Später, Jeff Labrum

17 December 1969, Portland

Dearest Rod,

Well, from what I read it's "bloody cold" over there. Are you getting used to it? We're praying for you Dear. . . .

Mom

19 *Dezember* 1969, Salzburg

Frohe Weihnachten, Bruder Saxey,

I've finally begun to settle down a bit after all the hassle of arriving. The first night here we taught a 2nd (discussion) to 5 student girls and a fellowshipping lesson to a newly baptized member. We have a really strong *Gemeinde* here, lots of priesthood holders. The work is harder than I expected, but I get a real kick out of it, especially when we teach someone golden. Most of our contacts are students. Keep up the good work and we'll see each other at conference sometime.

Merry Christmas! Br. Duke

20 *Dezember* 1969, Wels

Dear Mom & Dad,

Well, here it is, another cold day in the steppes of central Austria. It's been snowing again and it is pretty deep. That isn't so bad; it's the thawing (that turns) it all to muck on the streets. The bicycles kick it up on the pants legs, and passing trucks are not noted for courtesy.

Our total hours worked this week were pretty poor, about 60, but we have had remarkable success in getting into houses. We gave a First Discussion to a young family on Monday. He said ahead of time that we would have no success with him. He was right, he could not accept the apostasy. He did invite us back though for a further discussion and we're quite hopeful that something will touch him. In any case, that went pretty well. We had another visit with the three ladies. They are really golden, took the 1st with no problem, and we'll teach them the 2nd after Christmas. We contacted them through a "death-letter". We write introductory letters to families with new children or deaths, and then visit them. It is about the only time people ever think of anything except materialism.

We have one other investigator. He is the clerk in a bookstore I was looking through. He happened to have a book on Etruscan art out, I looked at it, mentioned my major of Archaeology, and it was just a logical progression to the Book of Mormon. I gave a pamphlet about the book to him, but it looks dismal for teaching because he lives so far away.

We met an interesting fellow the day before yesternight. He says he's over 70; has been all over Europe; speaks several languages—his English is pretty good; and spent about 12 years in various armies through the war. He was a medic, spent quite a bit of time in Italy (apparently Italian is his best foreign language), and saw a lot of misery. He is not bitter about the war, life, and everything, like so many people in Europe, but rather enjoys life.

We four missionaries went to a Christmas dinner celebration at Sister Rotheneder's. Her husband is bitter against the Church, so this was the only time we could come (when he wasn't there). I have not had so much to eat for a long time. Soup (great soups here), salad, chicken with rice, fruit salad, cookies (not as good as yours, though) and Christmas cake—wow!

Yesterday was our free day, so we worked in the morning in order to go to Linz in the evening and see *My Fair Lady*. That was really great, even in German. . .

Oh, the apartment was so nice and warm, but now our *Hausfrau* is "*lufting*". Oh, the cold!

Love, Rod

We grew very fond of Sister Reisenbichler. She was a little lady, only a little over four feet tall, with tidy grey hair, very thick "Coke bottle" glasses, and traditional, *echt Osterreichisch* (authentic Austrian) manners. Fresh air was important for health, so every day she would air out the apartment, no matter how cold the blizzard outside; she would use a washrag to chase away bits of smoke from the coal stove in the kitchen, which combined with her thick glasses and slow steps to form a very amusing picture. If we came home in the afternoon or early evening we would find her sitting in the kitchen, sipping herbal tea, and listening dreamily to Austrian "oldies" on the radio—music of the zither, accordion, or band, with songs in dialect and yodeling. She always treated us very kindly, like her own children.

She was particular about use of the stove, however. It was the only source of heat in the apartment and she did not want us lighting a fire in it. That meant there was no heat until she got up, which was about when we left for morning tracting or meetings. There were some mornings when it was so cold that when the alarm went off one of us would reach over, turn on the light, and say, "Good morning, Comp," followed by a similar reply. We would then stay in bed for our morning study class, fur hats on heads and scarves around our necks, our breath coming out in great clouds of vapor as we read scriptures to each other or discussed the gospel. Our milk stayed fresh without refrigeration, and froze if we stored it in the compartment between the bay windows.

Riding our bikes across town to meet with the other missionaries took about twenty minutes. By the time we arrived, our faces, hats, and scarves were covered with frost and on one occasion there was a half inch icicle hanging from the end of my nose.

23 December 1969, Portland

Dearest Rod,

. . . We were so happy to hear Edward's voice last night. It was after 10pm. We had been trying to get him from the time the first broadcast came on at before noon. You heard of course a plane crashed into the Naval Bldg in Miramar wrecking 4-5 F4s and killing 14 naval officers and injuring at least 30 others. Edward said he was in the restroom and when the crash came he grabbed his pants and ran. Two of his buddies I guess were killed and 2 or 3 more in the hospital. It was a horrible ordeal. Thank God Edward is okay! . . .

Mom

Culture shock is now a familiar concept, the difficulty people have adjusting to different customs and manners of life in a different land among foreign people, especially those habits of life and outlook that are taken for granted. Of course, shock is most severe when Westerners find themselves suddenly among tribal people or vice versa, something anthropologists train long and hard for, but still find difficult. Americans transplanted to European nations more typically experience a "culture burn"—that is, life is similar to what they are accustomed to at home, but different enough that annoyances sneak up on you. In my case, our family culture was still close enough to our Bavarian ancestors that adjusting to Austria was rapid and relatively comfortable.

There was, however, the unexpected, very European pessimism, an outlook so common that it is taken for granted by them, but can discourage a young American used to optimistic, positive, hopeful people. Understanding the causes of the gloom may be rapid for the mind, but takes time for the heart. World War II had made many resistant to the appeals of religion ("How could God let such things happen?") and the on-going tension of the Cold War fostered a deep-seated cynicism. At first this struck me as foolish, but over time my heart grew soft and my eyes moist as I began to understand more of what our Austrian, German, and Eastern European cousins had suffered. If only they might feel the power of the

Atonement through the Spirit, it would surely bring them joy and relief of pain.

The strengthening power of the Spirit was noticeable among our dear members, who, besides the general trial of war and postwar conditions, also had to endure varying degrees of prejudice and sometimes persecution because of their religion. The *Kirchensteuer*, for instance, was a tax collected by the state from all workers which was then paid to the Catholic Church for its support. It was possible to petition not to pay, but that was frowned upon by officials in a country where the governing political party and 90% of the population are nominally Catholic (even though the vast majority rarely goes to mass, if ever). There were exceptions, of course, but by and large our members labored on, patiently setting examples of faithfulness, helping one another, and extending great kindness to us. That kindness was often gustatory. If my letters and journal entries dwell disproportionately on food, it must have been because the food was so good—it seemed all the sisters, and many brethren, were excellent cooks. And yes, every Austrian cook bakes *Apfelstrudel*; they all make it differently; and they all are good.

26 *Dezember* 1969, Wels

Dear Mom & Dad,

. . . Christmas Eve we spent here at Sister Reisenbichler's. We had *Bratwürstl* (a kind of link sausage) and sauerkraut with apple juice to drink and a kind of bread called *Steyrbrot*. Later we had cookies and then went into the other room and lit the candles and sparklers on the tree. That was pretty neat. Later in the evening I read long and diligently in the third volume of the Trilogy (Br.

Welker gave it to me; he had two). We were stuffed. Earlier we visited Sister Kapp, who loaded us up with goodies. Br. Archibald gave me a fancy bookmark. He and I gave the other two missionaries a cake.

The next afternoon we had brunch—an American one: bacon and eggs and pan-fried toast and apple juice (no milk available). Sister Reisenbichler thinks we're crazy, eating that kind of stuff, 'says the toast is hard. In fact, their wonderful bread makes the best toast I have ever tasted, but no one here toasts it except crazy Americans. That evening we called on the *Familie* Darhuber, who gave us a supper of sausage, boiled eggs (struggling greatly, I downed them) and pickles, and a fruit tea. And they gave us a monstrous amount of candy and cookies. I have never been so stuffed in my life—and this noon we have another appointment— egad, I will be so fat!

The food here is really great. They have all sorts of herb and fruit teas we can drink. I will send a bunch home so you all can try them. We only have milk at home, when we buy it ourselves. Water is served if you ask for it, but not otherwise (they think the water is not healthful to drink, but I think it tastes excellent). The usual non-alcoholic drinks are fruit juices, of which there is a great variety, apple, raspberry, strawberry, and others I don't know the translation of. There are lots of soft drinks too.

The first of the week was really cold (-27 degrees C), but now it's somewhat warmer. Everything is really pretty—lots of snow, and all the trees white with frost. . .

Depending on what we're doing, we meet maybe 70-100 people per day. That's when we're tracting, but we try to avoid that because it's so unfruitful. The receptions vary, of course. Some are quite aggressive, slamming doors, etc.; some are chicken, look through their peep hole and don't say anything; some are friendly but content in ignorance or afraid of hearing something different; some are defiant, "I dare you to tell me something I don't already know"; some are not interested in religion; some are friendly and will listen because we're Americans and they want to try out their English; some want to debate scriptures; and then there are some, not many mind you, but some, who are friendly and want to hear because they really want to learn something. They are the Golden Ones.

It's rough in Wels. Everyone, nearly, knows who we are already and have already closed their minds. The town is about half Catholic and half Lutheran. . . There is much hypocrisy. Then, too, not only are the regular churches a problem, but so are the Jehovah's Witnesses, who are quite strong in Europe, but are not recognized by the Austrian government, so if they are caught tracting they can go to jail (the LDS Church has been officially recognized since 1955; some of our earlier missionaries were jailed as well).

Despite all the obstacles, we've got several great investigators now. We have one guy named Hager, who is really interesting. He wants all six discussions really quick, probably so he can say, "See, I told you, you couldn't convert me!" But we hope he will humble himself enough to feel the Spirit.

You asked about the language—now there is a story and a half. Austrian German is not much like High German, so slurred and full of idiosyncrasies. The first week or two were pretty rough trying to understand anyone, but now it generally goes okay, as long as they don't go too deep into dialect. Then too, people here make mistakes just like Americans. For instance, Sis. Reisenbichler is always getting her accusative and dative forms mixed up. And some of her plurals are just not right. A lot of people speak really clear and distinct High German, though, and that is when it goes easily.

On a normal day we have for breakfast 2 *Semmels* (little hard crusted rolls) with meat (*Wurst*) and /or cheese inside them, a *Krapfen* or two (round jelly-filled pastries), and a milk (1/2 liter) or a *fru-fru* (yogurt with fruit jam). We buy these at the *Konsum* or milk store. Sometimes we can get hot *Leberwurst* in the *Semmels*, and that's good. There are lots of kinds of *Wurst* and *Semmels*. Lunch is the big meal, and we generally have it at a *Gasthouse* (inn) or the *Donau Kaufhaus* (department store) or the *Wienerwald* (our favorite restaurant). Usually we have something like a Wienerschnitzel or fried pork with *Knödel* (dumpling), or goulash, or fried fish, or something like that. Supper is usually about the same as breakfast.

. . . I bought a "Braun" electric shaver the other day for $24-I decided this business of shaving with cold water on cold mornings is for the birds. . . Here is Br. Archibald:

"Greetings from the most ornery companion in all of Austria! Well, I'd just like to tell you what a privilege it is working with your son. We're having a great time for Christmas and I'm sure I'll not forget this one for as long as I live! Br. Saxey and I are meeting some wonderful people and we're going to try to our best to baptize some of them. Best wishes for the coming year of 1970!

Sincerely, Elder John F. Archibald"

2 January 1970, Wels

Dear Mom & Dad,

On the 31st we all went to Linz and worked with the brethren there—no proselyting, just visiting the members. That evening we spent at the branch party there. The Linz *Gemeinde* is really sharp—large, with lots of young people, and meeting in an honest to goodness church house rather than in just a little locale like we have here in Wels. When the clock passed 12 the four of us were in the middle of the large and at that time very empty *Hauptbahnhof* Linz, waiting for the train to Wels to arrive. We also spent some time at the top of the front steps there looking at all the sky rockets going off over the town—fireworks are legal here. The next day we were invited out—noon at Sr. Kapp's and evening at the Darhuber's. Were we ever stuffed after 6 *Knödel*, a portion of venison, a portion of rabbit *schnitzel*, 2 portions of compote, 2 salads, 2 soups, and innumerable cookies. It was a repetition of Christmas.

. . . Br. Fagar and I were working together on Monday and tracted out an interesting character. The fellow is about 60 years old. When he was young he was strong Catholic, but along about thirty became disenchanted, seeing the mess the world was in. He investigated other churches at the time but it all seemed a mass of confusion to him. He decided the only order was in nature and so, claiming there is no god, he looks to nature as the higher order and claims to have eternal life in that he is a part of the eternal circle of nature. He was quite adamant about it and obviously we got nowhere with him.

It gets pretty discouraging at times, seeing investigators fall away, getting doors slammed in the face, watching members misbehave. The most depressing part though is from the other missionaries, some of whom tend to be quite negative, especially the old ones. They really need a jolt of Pres. Wood enthusiasm. . .

Love, Rod

I enjoyed working with Br. Fagar. He was a thin young Idaho cowboy with angular features and a sense of humor that went on and on. We sometimes had contests telling jokes and tall tales, or seeing who could do the most pushups before turning in for the night. He was an excellent missionary.

7 January 1970, Wels

Dear Mom & Dad,

. . . Things are pretty well normal here. We had a snow at the first of the week. It was really cold Monday, but then a *Föhn* (Chinook wind) came and now the snow is almost all gone and temperatures are into the high 40s. Today is clear and we're planning on getting a few pictures. At noon, we have an appointment with Herr Wist to visit the museum (finally). The only trouble with that is missing dinner and having a hard time finding time to bathe.

This has been an interesting week. We haven't done much teaching—only 2.5 hours (last week was 5.5 hours), but have gotten into quite a few interesting discussions. It's remarkable how many people, particularly older ones, do not believe in God, but say they have God in Nature. We talked to one man about 15 minutes at the door. He kept raging along about no God, God is Nature, religion is like politics, and so forth, until finally I got sort of perturbed and asked him why he doesn't open his eyes. It was about that time he changed from "*du-Sprache*" (used for children and animals) to "*Sie-Sprache*" (used for adults). We bore strong testimony, which stopped him cold. We gave him some tracts and told him to read them. He mumbled "auf wiedersehen" and turned, a glazed look in his eyes.

We taught a man a 1st discussion last night. He really

seems golden and we're hopeful for him. That other lady, the one we found by inspiration tracting isn't moving too quickly. We are having a hard time finding her at home, but are looking forward to being able to teach her when we do.

We have met many people this week who are afraid of us. It is remarkable how these people actually fear the presence of two 20 year old boys. Sometimes they'll just look through the little holes in the doors, and, recognizing who we are, walk away without saying a word.

It is clearer to me now why they had the big apostasy here last year. They lost four really strong families at that time. Gradually, bits of information from that time, and a few problems since then, are coming out. Br. Duke and I feel like detectives (the other two brethren haven't quite got it yet). Hopefully, though, we may eventually find out what happened. . . .

'Bye, Rod

I never did find out exactly what it was that caused the problems in the branch. In the end it did not matter. People in every society have their conflicts, often over trivial matters or personality differences. The challenge is to learn to love and forgive and cooperate despite our differences, a lesson which was taught to me with particular sharpness towards the end of my mission.

9 January 1970, Portland

My Dearest,

. . . Yesterday it was a sheet of ice from I guess The Dalles to Medford and north thru Seattle—silver thaw! Dad got me to work and Clyde (Waddell) got me home. I wasn't about to drive on it. It's raining today; I never liked the rain so much as I did today. . . . Mom

9 January 1970, Wels

Dear Mom & Dad,

. . . Things are starting to get back to normal now. Br. Archibald has had a cold and so we've had to stay at home, even though there are no holidays (well, Tuesday was the day of Three Kings, but missionaries don't count as many holidays as the Austrians). We sure haven't been getting much done; and our hours are way down. My feeling in this regard apparently is starting to get across to the other brethren, though, and I think things will start shaping up.

The other night we went to teach the three ladies I told you about. We went to give a Second Discussion and introduce the Book of Mormon, but it took an hour just to give the review. They just weren't accepting the fact that man needs to do more than just pray and be nice. They admitted the Catholic Church is false; indeed they complain vociferously about their church, and yet they say, "Why change?" So we used the next hour just to work on this problem rather than the discussion. I don't know if they felt the Spirit or not, but Br. A and I sure did. We reasoned, testified, "*schlaged*" (cited scriptures), and warned in the strongest words I have ever heard used with investigators. We got a comeback for next week, so hopefully they will do a little real praying on this point so we can continue. Rather than give them a Second Discussion, we'll probably give a Fifth (the Plan of Salvation) instead. Then perhaps they'll begin to realize there are a few differences between our respective beliefs.

One of our three regular places to eat is a little *Gasthaus* near where the other two missionaries live. The innkeeper is a really great old Hungarian we call "Pete". He speaks pretty good English and really likes us. Our first time there we had a great venison goulash. Now it's such that when he comes over and recommends something he dashes off to the kitchen and brings us a big sample. The other day I was having a pork cutlet with *Knödel* and Br. Archibald a noodle and kraut dish. I mentioned I would probably order the noodle and kraut dish next time because it looked so good. So he dashed off to the kitchen and brought me a big dish of it. I tried to pay him for it, but he wouldn't take it. He is really great. One of these days we will have to try and interest him in the Church.

There is a big church right near here. It was built in the 9th century and is in really good shape, a beautiful little example of late Romanesque architecture. The decoration inside is beautiful, though I imagine pretty plain compared to the one in Taxco, Mom. (She often spoke affectionately of her visit to her brother Hal and his family in Mexico.) . . . John Smurthwaite writes that things are really moving in Italy; he is in Torino. . . Rod

14 January 1970, San Diego

Dear Rod,

. . . Edward left Saturday for a pre-cruise exercise period in the Caribbean. He'll be home in March and then leaves again in April till December. It's going to be a long year. . . .

Lynn

16 January 1970, Wels

Dear Mom & Dad,

. . . The fruitcake arrived in fine condition and is really good. The *Butterkuchen* were pretty thoroughly broken up, but the *Springerle* and the *Lebkuchen* came through just great and really taste good. The authentic European *Lebkuchen* can't compare to ours. Thank you.

I slipped on the ice and came flying across the pavement with my bike on me last week. The only damage was a great hole in the knee of my new suit. Sr. Kapp repaired it for me and it looks pretty good—evidence that I am an experienced missionary: a patched suit.

My glasses finally gave up the ghost the other day and the frames broke at the nose piece where they had been cracked long ago. I took them to a place downtown and had the lenses changed over to my old frames.

Our work is improving. For the first time since I have been here we are going to get a week with a decent number of hours worked-65 for this one. My companion can't believe we're actually achieving this goal so well. He hasn't had a 65 hour week in 6-8 months. I am sure seeing a goal achieved will help a great deal towards improving the attitudes around here.

We had an interesting experience Tuesday night. We had eaten dinner and still had an hour to use before visiting the family Eidherr. Br. Fagar, another greenie, and I were working together. Since my German is better and we were working our area, I was acting Senior. I decided to go to a few comebacks in our immediate vicinity. We went to one house, but it was locked and there was no bell, so we couldn't get in. We started to go to another when Br. Fagar suggested we try being led by the Spirit, like the great missionaries of old. We prayed, walked down the street, prayed again, and both had a feeling we ought to try the *Stiege* across the street. We went up several flights, looking carefully at the names on the doors as we passed. Finally we stopped at a landing, prayed, and decided to go back to the last door we had passed. We introduced ourselves and were invited right in by a Herr Barth. He showed considerable interest and we made an appointment with him. He is a well educated English teacher. Considering the usual ratio of slammed doors, no interest, no faith, to golden contacts, this is certainly to be reckoned as a manifestation of the Spirit.

In any case, life goes on pretty normally here in Eiselsberg; or, at least, as normally as can be expected when you're living halfway in the 19th century—wearing suspenders and vests, riding trolley cars, only heat a coal stove in the kitchen, no refrigeration except that which occurs naturally, having to help a good sister down the street work her hand pump for water, seeing a horse-drawn barrel cart go down the street, enjoying the smell of coal smoke in the air and having black coal-rings on the collars of our white shirts every day, and just in general living in a bygone age—for good and for bad.

Love, Roderick Sarey

p.s. We've been studying old German script as part of our effort to arouse interest by impressing people.

It was uncommon to encounter Muslims, and incredibly rare to have the chance to teach them, since Islam forbids conversion and according to many of their leaders is punishable by death, so the following note from Don was intriguing.

18 January 1970, Berlin

Dear Rod,

. . . Right now we are teaching a golden Moslem. He knew Nasser personally, but was imprisoned because he did a study on the equipment Egypt was buying from the USSR and said that it was outdated and of poor quality. He was trying to help his country, but they didn't like his report. He is now here in Berlin.

I just heard that Pres. McKay died. Shock!

Love, Your *Bruder*, Don B. Waddell

Chapter 6

20 January 1970, At sea just south of Cuba

Dear Ricky,

Well we are at it again, playing games and spending the taxpayers' money. Those of us who flew aboard left Miramar the 10th, stopped at Tinker AFB, just outside of Oklahoma City, then flew to NAS Key West Florida. We stayed the night in Key West then flew to NAS Leeward Point in Guantanamo Bay, Cuba, the next day. . . . After trapping (landing aboard) we started carrier qualifications. These consist of launching and recovering aboard as soon as possible to get the landing practice. . . . Last year I got 65 traps on the *Enterprise*, so I'm hoping to get over 100 this year on the *America* so I'll be eligible for a centurion patch . . .

Friday evening we put back into port in Gitmo (Guantanamo Bay). . . . (T)oday we are out with very little flying for the F-4s, but are conducting general quarter drill, etc.

We were originally going to go into St. Thomas, an island just East of Puerto Rico, but that is just tentative. So far, things are just as they are always—all screwed up! Am really looking forward to going home for the month of March. This is really getting old. . . .

Love, Edward

23 January 1970, Wels

Dear Mom & Dad,

Well, this has been a most eventful week. Br. Archibald was transferred to Wien (he spent his first 7.5 mos. there and hates it) and Br. Duke, my good friend from the LTM came down from Salzburg. He and I are Co-Juniors. This is really going to be great—we'll work well together.

I am glad about your callings, Mom. That Teacher Training Class is sharp, and you will have all sorts of fun with it. Doing this kind of work is the true way to happiness—in the service of God and our fellowmen.

Most of the people here seem so unhappy. . . Much of this sense of emptiness can be attributed to the wars, of course. Much, however, must also be accounted for by the Catholic Church. The Church has a terrific hold. It is like an old rotten tree stump with great roots clutching at the soil. . . Those who listen, though, and accept the Gospel, are changed as if by magic. The true church is indeed a Church of Miracles, miracles in the lives of the members. . . .

We spoke with a man the other day, a high school teacher. He says he's an atheist. He views religions as an answer to a psychological need, one from which he has freed himself. Of course, we could get nowhere with him, for we had no basis of agreement from which to start. And as we spoke, I thought, even as we can get nowhere with him because of his unbelief, so he can get nowhere with himself.

Another, rather belligerent man we spoke with repeatedly asked who and what Christ was. I told him about the godhead and the plan of salvation. He became angry with me, saying he wanted a "modern church", one without all these old "myths about Christ." In other words, he wanted a church that taught what he already believed in, whether true or not. (See 2 Tim 4:3-4)

This transfer was interesting. We put Br. Archibald on the 9:45 train, helping him aboard with his bags. Br. Fagar was worried about not getting off in time so he left early. Br. Mauchley and I, however, were half-way down the hall when we felt the surges of power go through the train, indicating it was starting up. We dropped the bags and high-tailed it for the entrance, but the conductor barred the way (in truth we were moving slowly enough to have jumped with no danger). So, we had an unexpected and rather expensive (fined) trip to Linz. We didn't get back until noon, all the other trains being delayed. We talked with an American in Linz, gave him a few tracts, so maybe we were supposed to go to Linz after all.

Today is Saturday. Yesterday evening we finally got together with Herr Wist. He is really a neat guy, well read and studied. We gave him a Book of Mormon and a rather poor version of a great B of M *vortrag* (slide presentation) we have called *Stimme aus dem Staube* (Voices From the Dust). He was really taken aback by what we said. "Astonished," quoth he. He'll do okay. . .

Love, Rod

I tended to be quite critical of the Catholic Church, at least partly because I had never before lived in a country with an established, state religion, but also because at first I felt a certain adversarial relationship. That feeling changed over time as I came to appreciate better the deep faith and devotion of many good Catholics, not to mention the exquisite works of music, art, and architecture that individuals had been inspired to create through the centuries, and the exquisite good works of living saints such as Mother Theresa of Calcutta. The devotion to freedom demonstrated by Pope John Paul II and his working relationship with Ronald Reagan and Margaret Thatcher in bringing about the fall of the Soviet Empire solidified my appreciation for the Catholic Church, notwithstanding doctrinal differences. We have much in common and are not adversaries after all.

26 January 1970, Portland

Dearest Son,

Your Father became an Elder Sunday and he kept it a secret until they had him stand up in Sacrament. He's been working hard at the Superintendant job in Sunday School and I'm pleased; I'm sure you are. . . .

Sis. Howard talked at Sacrament Sunday telling of her experiences and how so many missionaries gave her up as a lost cause but that the 7th and 8th missionaries were the successful ones, so don't you and Br. A be discouraged at so short a time. And remember too, Rod, how many your Mother gave a bad time to. So you see, 4 missionaries in Sunnyside—Dear Br. Tree, Guy Patterson, and umpteen others!!!

. . . Mom

30 January 1970, Wels

Dear Mom & Dad,

Well, this has been an interesting week. We've met a remarkable number of people and made many appointments, though most of them have fallen through.

Monday night it was getting rather late (people go to bed early here) when we passed a lady on the street. We had the feeling we should talk to her, so I approached and bore testimony. She really wasn't too interested, but did respond, so we went up to her apartment and taught the first part of the First Discussion. She gave us chamomile tea (tastes vaguely like Seven Stars Tea) and cookies. She did not respond so terribly well, but we'll go back and give her a chance.

Thanks a lot for the pictures—I had looked forward to getting them. . . Be sure you write "Austria" on the envelope. The last one said "Australia" and took a long cut through Sydney. . . .

The new suit is dark blue with a sort of red-gold stripe in it. I really like it—too bad to think two years from now it'll be pretty well *kaput*. They're having closeout sales now, and I wish I could afford something. I saw a *Steyrmark* suit (authentic traditional Austrian grey with green trim) for only $24. Of course, now would be the wrong time to get that sort of thing. Next year will be better. As far as finances go, $100 is more than adequate for the usual month. . . .

We had a wonderful meal at Schwester Kapp's at noon: noodle-rabbit soup, Russian salad (very sour), sour pickles, rabbit goulash with potatoes, and two *Semmel Knödel*, apple-prune compote, and baked goodies. We had strawberry juice to drink and were so stuffed! . . . Fridays are especially great days, because of baths in the afternoon. . . No time to read them, but I did purchase two paperback books here, a collection of references of Socrates and a book of myths.

I love you, Rod

8 February 1970, Portland

Dear Rod,

    . . . I get a brief "rundown" on you each Sunday and enjoy the progress you are making riding a bike in the winter. Sounds great! What, no Ramblers? They picked a good winter to initiate you into your new calling, but then just think of the stories you can tell one day to our Priest Quorum.

    We sure have a room full of priests—about nine active ones. Then we have an average of 24 to our Sunday School class. Several non-members are attending and they are coming great. Debbie Ward has been bringing a young man who has taken the discussions but his parents won't let him be baptized. Last Sunday at fast and testimony meeting (one of our very best) nearly the entire meeting was taking up with great young people's testimonies. Most of them were 14-17 years of age. Suddenly at the end of the meeting this boy, Debbie's friend, got up, walked to the pulpit, and spent about 10 minutes telling us about his love and testimony of the Gospel. He was tremendous. The Bishop closed the meeting and all of the youth flooded over to him "hugging" and "crying"—it was great. A real spirit of love and testimony was shared by all.

    . . . Jeff is taking German (at BYU). I think he is "planning ahead" hoping to be your companion this summer. He will go on his mission as quickly as school lets out. He turns 19 on 24 May. Randy Rowley will also go this spring. . . .

    Your folks are doing real well. I see them each Sunday. Your Dad is really growing in his Sunday School job and your Mom seems pleased to be included in some way. . . .

    I know you are a dedicated missionary and working very

hard—that is your nature. May I suggest that in your hard work you take some time each day to think and meditate. Do it with a pencil in your hand. Reflect back on your attitude (positive), your methods of finding, follow-up, and teaching. How can you improve? Is there a better, more productive way? As you give these questions, and others, some consideration, on a regular basis, the Lord will inspire you with even greater success.

Please know that our thoughts and prayers are with you. . . Our prayers will continue to be for your good health and success.

Your friend, Pres. Wood

13 February 1970, Wels

. . . Herr Wist is coming with considerable difficulty. He is exceedingly well educated and studied. He will not recognize that prophets speak for God. He knows so much of the background material for the Bible that he can explain away even the clearest scriptures. That is aggravating. We pray for him.

Bruder Fagar and I tried "inspiration tracting" one night and went right to a Herr Barth. We have an appointment to teach him on the 16th. Another time we found Frau Thalhuber, about whom we are hopeful, though she is coming along with difficulty. In any case, we know that when we put ourselves sufficiently in tune with the Spirit, He can and will guide us in the work.

13 February 1970, Wels

Dear Mom and Dad,

Thank you for the sweater-vests. They are beautiful and the fit is excellent! . . . About aerogrammes: I've used them a few times, but here they cost 20 cents, so I'm not really saving much (price of paper and envelopes), though they do limit your writing space, which is sometimes a good thing. . .

We met twice this week with Herr Wist, the bookstore worker. He knows so much about history and philosophy that it is almost impossible to do anything with him. When we quote a scripture he goes into an analysis of it—stylistic, where it came from, etc. He won't accept anything the way it's written. He also seems unwilling to pray about Joseph Smith and the *Book of Mormon*. . .

At the moment we are leisurely cooking French toast. It is really great. We are lucky to be able to do any cooking. Not many *Wohnungs* have such an opportunity. That really improves the diet. Austrians don't eat vegetables in winter, at least not hot ones. So we get canned beans, peas, etc. I can't tell if I'm gaining or losing weight. We have no scale. Today we get to bathe. That is good; things get pretty old after a week.

The presidency of each prophet has been characterized by certain accomplishments in the building of the Church. Joseph Smith, of course, was the Restoration; Brigham Young, the migration; Lorenzo Snow, tithing; Heber J. Grant, the Welfare Program; David O. McKay, growth; and so forth. Considering the waves and movement being felt in the Church now, all indicating streamlining for the last great push before the Millennium, one wonders what will characterize Pres. Smith's term in office.

John Smurthwaite writes that the work is moving well in Italy. Last year the Italian Mission had over 300 baptisms (Austria about 150). It is prophesied that the day will come when Italy will lead all Europe in conversions; indeed, the Church will one day be surpassingly strong there on the Pope's own doorstep. . . . Rod

13 Feb 1970, About 70 miles north of St. Thomas, Virgin Islands

Dear Ricky,

. . . Our squadron had a few A/C at NAS Roosevelt Rhoads in Puerto Rico that had to be flown out to the ship Tuesday so a buddy of mine and I volunteered. So (we flew commercially) to San Juan Monday evening. We went to a fabulous restaurant/night club for dinner and show. They had flamenco dancers. . .

Since then we have been running what we call cyclic ops. That is 12 hours flying, 12 hours off. Flight quarters usually sound about 0745 and the last launch secures usually about 2100. Add running our shops and standing watches makes for long days. But that way they pass reasonably quickly. Today was a particularly bad day which might make people even more superstitious for Friday the 13th. We had several (5) very large JP5 spills, one resulting in a fire on the 03 level and CAT-2, one A-7 had a hook nitrogen bottle explode on landing which caused a fire and 3 of our A/C experienced in -flight emergencies. But the flying day is over and everybody is safe, and on top of that the ship's chaplain is riding with us tomorrow.

We are going to be operating in this area through the 26th or so of February, then fly off for Miramar (San Diego) with stops in Florida and Texas for fuel. The non-flying personnel in the squadron aren't so lucky as they will have to wait till the ship puts into Navy Mayport (near Jacksonville, Florida) before they can get off to fly back to San Diego. We will spend all of March in San Diego and start moving the squadron early in April to Norfolk . . .

Take care, Ricky, but have fun, ok? I'll expect you to be an expert skier when you get back. Till next time. . . . Edward

Skiing was against mission rules, much to Br. Archibald's disappointment. It was not against the rules for the local school-children, though, and we frequently saw very young children ski-ing or ice-skating their way to school with large packs of books on their backs.

15 February 1970, Wels

. . . Missionary life is strange at times . . . It is a Zwischenleben, a "between life". We are between two languages, between two cultures, between two religions (in several senses, between Catholicism and Mormonism in Austria, between Christ's Church and all the others, between a self religion and an other's religion, and between the religious Mormon life as it is practiced back home and as it is practiced here). And the young missionary must sort it out.

I was quite satisfied with the "me" of before-mission time. I expected changes, but did not desire any basic ones. I was very proud of my past accomplishments and naturally desire to remain the same sort of person who accomplished them. And yet, it is a fact that with every thought or act we change to become someone new.

. . . I tend to be overly critical of others and overly sensi-tive to unintentional hurts. . . I feel frustrated at not remembering facts I once knew (not surprising since I have studied nearly noth-ing other than language and religion for the last five months). This is chewing away at my confidence . . . Apparently I am being test-ed. I am in need of humility, understanding, and patience. . .

15 February 1970, Wels

Dear Rod,

. . . Your letters indicate a little impatience on your part with the "heathen". Please be patient and do not forget that it took your Mother 30 years and your Father as long to become an Elder. Someone has said that you really become a missionary when you can truthfully say that you love the people regardless of their imperfections. . . .

(Our new company, *Chemtron*, has been making progress, providing reagents to laboratories.) I hope you are collecting a lot of slides of the area and the people. You should try to make a pictorial record of your mission.

The Sunday School is becoming more complex—more meetings. As always, a few people do all the work. Every Sunday someone asks about you. . . .

May God bless you, Your Father

19 February 1970, Portland

Dear Mom & Dad,

Our nice weather didn't last very long. No sooner were the streets dry when it began to snow again. Now we have about a half foot and still coming down. The weather has really been weird here: one time we had warm sun, snow, rain, and hail all in the same day. . . .

Well, we've bathed and had our haircuts now and feel thoroughly refreshed. Also, Friday is our day for French toast, which settled most satisfactorily. Two letters came, one from each of you. Thank you. Sorry if I sounded too negative. I'm really not—indeed, of the missionaries I've met, I'm one of the most un-negative (I'm not so daring as to say positive). One problem is that if I'm to write about successful mission experiences, I have to have some first.

. . . We met with Herr Wist again and talked all night. He's a neat fellow . . . but isn't yielding easily to the enticing of the Gospel. For me, he is a particularly interesting fellow because we are remarkably alike, the primary differences attributable to Americanism and the Gospel.

Remember Herr Barth, whom Br. Fagar and I found about a month and a half ago by "inspiration tracting"? Br. Duke and I taught him the other night. We did not get far with the discussion, he only wanted to talk, but maybe we planted a few seeds.

Br. Duke and I were walking home from town the other night talking about "leftism" when I felt very strongly we should go back and try a few of the "come-backs" in the area we had just started. The come-back we picked had been made about a month earlier. We went up and talked to the lady briefly and she seemed quite interested. She then loaned us a book she had (published in 1854) which talked about the Mormons. Perhaps she won't be converted, but at least we're bound to sow a few more seeds. That feeling to go back came straight out of the blue. Do strange and unexpected things ever happen on missions?

We went into a Catholic Order School the other day and taught a Catholic missionary (leaving shortly for Brazil) about the *Book of Mormon*. He'll talk to the Headmaster now and hopefully we'll get to speak to a few of the classes. It's a high school and we're really excited at the prospect of giving them a presentation.

Every day we meet so many fascinating and different people. If I sound distressed about them at times it's only because I wish a few more would listen to us and have the joy of the Gospel come into their lives. The typical replies we get when we introduce ourselves on the door (if we get to do that before they slam it) are "no interest" or "no time". No interest in the Gospel of Jesus Christ! No time for the one thing in the universe that can bring true joy in one's life! No, I don't think ill of these people, I do not curse them. But I do cry a little. Satan has worked heavily upon them, confused them, and frightened them. If they knew what they were doing, then perhaps I could have a feeling against them, but not while they remain in ignorance.

There is, of course, a certain amount of "culture shock", which perhaps is better described as "culture burn". But for me at least, this has proven no great problem, being pretty well prepared for it in German class and at home. . .

Auf wiedersehen, Rod

20 February 1970, Wels

We met again with Herr Wist. He was fascinated with the Pre-existence, but still doesn't believe that there is an absolute truth and that prophets dispense this truth to the people. I really think he will eventually understand and believe. . . .

Bruder Duke and I attended mass tonight. We both perceived the emptiness and hollowness of it all. The ritual, the robes, everything, was as an empty form of something once alive, but now dead. It is rather like certain science fiction stories where the culture is destroyed, but the remnants are revered as holy. This church is but a vestige of the Church of Christ which worshipped the true and living God.

Afterwards we spoke with the priest about the church. We

asked a number of questions, the answers to which were quite re-
vealing, for instance: "Were you called to the priesthood? No. It
just seemed like a good job for which he was suited. Does the Pope
receive revelation? No." We asked about the organization of the
church. Our impression was that he did not really believe it him-
self. No wonder there are so few in attendance.

I occasionally had bouts of abdominal pain during this time
period, but thought nothing of it. One day it was particularly
strong, doubling me over, so we went to the hospital. A very young
doctor asked me about the pain and said I probably had appendici-
tis and they should operate—all that without a physical exam or
blood work! I used the hospital phone to call President Broberg.
He asked about the pain and I told him it was low in the right low-
er abdomen. He replied in his excited voice, "That's not appendici-
tis! Get out of the hospital, go home, and go to bed." We obeyed
and I felt much better soon thereafter.

24 February 1970, Wels

Today was a pretty good day. We spoke about half an hour
with a lady at the door. She claimed not to believe in God, being
another victim of the War, which had a devastating effect on the
faith of so many of the people here. We bore such strong testimony
though, that she wept as we spoke. I think she would really like to
believe—she certainly felt the Spirit at that time—but is too afraid.
We have had many such experiences lately.

I feel within me so many feelings and am grappling with so
many thoughts . . . it is difficult to understand my role in it all. I
had heard that a mission was an opportunity for peace, when

things become resolved. I must say, however, that I was much more at peace before my mission than now. I am experiencing more turmoil and change than ever before.

24 February 1970, Portland

Dearest Rod,

You should see the lovely sunshine—all the camellias, forsythia, flowering quince, crocuses, and daffodils are blooming now, and the willow trees are a bright yellow-green with leaves. Spring is truly a delightful time of year.

Love, Mom

Letters from Mom typically discussed the plants and flowers in bloom, weather (always a matter of interest), social events, meals they had prepared for church or other groups, the dogs, and the activities of Wayne's children, their first grandchildren. This was a busy time in Wayne's life, working long hours and trying to raise a young family.

27 February 1970, Wels

Dear Mom and Dad,

Well, another week is by. For a couple days we had really nice weather—sunshine, warm, all snow gone. Last night the snow returned and we have now about 3 inches.

We met last night with Herr Wist. We tried to give a Third Discussion (how one perceives Truth), but he was so confused we couldn't continue. An hour was spent getting through the first three questions. Here is a person who has studied so much that, without a firm background in Truth, all which he has studied is jumbled together into a veil before his eyes so that he cannot perceive the real Truth when it comes. And, he is not humble enough to pray, without which action he will never find out what's true. We will have to drop him; there is no point in trying to continue to teach him—he is just not ready yet.

A more positive experience was had 2 days ago. We called back on a lady we had met tracting and were ushered right in. We achieved a common ground in rock and mineral collecting and work . . . and then proceeded to give a golden Second Discussion (*Book of Mormon* introduction). It was unbelievable—she gave book answers—the ones they are supposed to give—straight out of the book. She even quoted our scripture for us a page in the discussion before we got to it. Then, of all things, she even volunteered to read the *Book of Mormon* by next Tuesday. It was really great.

That same day we ate at Schwester Kapp's and I picked up a few more recipes from her. She talked about when she lived on the farm. There used to be a colony of dwarves (you can imagine what that did to me) which lived on the other side of the *Donau*. They used to come into the towns and dance with trained bears for money. She also related an experience of how once the gypsies came onto her farm and demanded food. She gave them some, but before leaving they also took her 18 month old son. She screamed for help and a nearby farmer came and scared them off. Some while later they found the son left on a haystack nearby. . . .

We told a Joseph Smith story to a lady the other day. She really came along well and will try to make a meeting for us with her husband. He is a retired author of historical novels and hunting books. We are hopeful on this one, also that we may get a lot of group meetings in the near future. . . .

Love, Rod

3 *März* 1970, *Wien*

Dear Br. Saxey and Br. Duke!

. . . Br. Feil and I are seeing a lot of teaching success here, but a couple of our best investigators have fallen through on us. We expect better things to come.

I know that you brethren are doing a fantastic job, so keep up the good work, *gel*?

Jeff Labrum
p.s. *Schöne Gruss von Bruder Feil* (Greetings from Brother Feil)

6 *März* 1970, Wels

Dear Mom & Dad,

. . . Br. Mauchley, our District Leader, was transferred to Salzburg and Br. Schurtleff took his place. As far as hours go, Br. Duke and I have been leading the District for the last 4 weeks. . . .

Wednesday, when we went to Linz for our study class, we found a drunk lady on the street, dazed, holding her bloodied hand. She said some man had hit her hand with a bottle, but it looked more like she had tried to slash her hands for suicide. We went to call the police, but the workmen at the construction site across the street said they had already done so. She didn't want any help, though we did prevail on a man there to makeshift a bandage. There wasn't much more we could do, so continued our walk, hailing down a police car a short distance away, to make sure official help got to her. The gory scene the woman presented—she had gotten blood all over herself—wasn't nearly as nauseating as that of the people around. People nearby laughed at her; one man we stopped for help said simply, "but I've got to get to work." . . .

At the moment, the wonderful fragrance of French toast fills the air. We are indeed fortunate to be able to cook. Not all missionaries have that opportunity. There's no maple syrup, but apricot jam is just as good or better.

We haven't any investigators at the moment. They've all "given us the ax", even that 'golden' second we taught. We've been giving out quite a few copies of the *Book of Mormon*, though, a lot of tracts, and done a little teaching, so we're hopeful that things will improve shortly. Almost two years ago Ezra Taft Benson was in Linz and said, "I see thousands of members of the Church here in Linz two years from now." Others have prophesied of a great advance at this present time, too. Also, our group of 18, the largest ever to come to Austria at one time, had a strong feeling of "specialness". The entire mission is young (in our district there is only one who has been here longer than five months) and is experiencing a sense of change. Indeed, there are currents in the Church generally which indicate great things are underway.

We spoke the other day with a Nazi. He was another of those who had been on the Russian Front (there are a lot of them around here). Unlike others we've met though, he seemed to miss the "good old days". In speaking of Moscow he said, "We almost made it. Only an Italian commander goofed. We almost made it!" He had quite a distaste for America, as do many people here.

Something that gets really perturbing is when they begin trying to tell us what it's like in America and what our history is.

This guy, for instance, would not accept that there had been anti-slavery laws before Kennedy. I almost lost my temper with him—we've got our problems in America, but things are a lot better than in Europe. But most of the people won't listen to us. After all, we were only born there.

We had dinner at the Darhuber's last Sunday. He got to knocking America too; that has been happening a lot lately, probably something to do with the elections. He was captured by the Russians on the Front. As usual, he was hitting the American bombing of Wels during the War. You know, I get so tired of hearing about something that happened 25 years ago! You can't talk to anybody over 30 for five minutes before they bring it up: "Oh, we experienced the War. Don't try and tell us about God." Experiences are supposed to be learned from, not used as a crutch for slothfulness and an excuse for ignorance. Anyway, it was a wonderful meal. (Sister Darhuber is a great cook.)

The Austrian elections are finally over—the Socialist Party won. Though obviously I am not in favor of socialism, I'm told this is better than the chief rival, the People's Party, which is synonymous with the Catholic Church. The latter has been in power the last five years and is blamed for higher prices, etc. Very few people like the C. Church here, even the Catholics. Every day we find several people who have left that church and, though their names are on the rolls, belong to no church. Of those who are Catholic, nearly all are so only because they were born one and you can't get an education or a job very well if you aren't one. The Catholic Church tax drives a lot of people from their church and is usually the only connection their members have with the church (overall attendance is about 3%).

I guess I've carried on enough for now, and I do hope it

doesn't sound negative enough to command the sending of a "cheer-up" letter. Be sure to send some pictures of Oregon, both sides of the Cascades. People are always asking what it's like where I live, and all I can say is, "like Salzburg". . .

Love, Rod

p.s. We had a great lunch from Sis. Reisenbichler. I haven't gotten the recipe yet, but will—bread crumbs, eggs, and raisins all fried together.

We were occasionally challenged about what America was doing in Vietnam, but were almost always able to get out of the exchange by correctly pleading ignorance. Our awareness was limited to what our family and friends mentioned in letters or what we happened to notice on headlines in the newsstands when we went by.

Race relations were a different matter because we knew something about the topic. Again, we generally avoided confrontation and tried to steer the conversation back to the gospel; Christ, after all, came to redeem all mankind, whatever the race or nationality. On one occasion, however, a particularly pointed attack by an angry man who had been in World War II became more than I could handle. "How can you justify the terrible treatment you give the blacks in your country?" he said again after a long tirade. I quietly responded that we are striving to improve things in America, that people in all countries have to learn to deal with ethnic and race differences peaceably, and then added, "There used to be a great many Jews in Germany." The conversation came to an amiable, but rapid close.

Hypocrisy is not limited to grumpy old men. Another time

in Wels we four missionaries were seated in a crowded restaurant. There was a group of fashionably dressed middle-aged ladies at the table next to us, discoursing to each other about the shocking bigotry and racial prejudice against blacks in America. We were relieved when they went on to another topic. Shortly later two Yugoslavians entered the room and were seated in the corner. The ladies took notice and the one who had been talking most critically about America scowled and leaned to her friends to whisper how awful it was to have to eat with them in the room.

Being American was not always held against us or a source of criticism; more often than not it was an advantage. Some would talk to us just for variety's sake or out of curiosity. While teaching a high school English teacher we were invited to sing the national anthem into a tape recorder for use in her class. Neither Br. Duke nor I were singers; besides, for the life of us we could not remember the words. We ended up singing *My Country Tis of Thee*. Poorly.

10 March 1970, Wels

Dear Mom & Dad,

. . . Spring is finally taking hold in Wels, despite occasional relapses into Winter. I don't know if I mentioned what a beautiful town this is. The air is clean, the architecture interesting, the buildings painted pleasant pastels; it is really great. Wednesday we worked in Linz, which is not nearly as pleasant as it is here.

Br. Duke and I are getting along well and relate very well. We had had some misunderstandings, but these have worked out and we're the best of friends. I love him dearly.

We have been taking advantage of our cooking facilities.

Last Sunday we had a steak dinner (Austrians don't usually eat steak) and during the week I fixed two big batches of eggs "Texas Style". The only problem is gaining weight. Egad!

We'll have an interview conference with Pres. Broberg on April 21. We heard General Conference in a telephone transmission in Linz.

Br. Duke has a copy of the German translation of *The Kingdom of God Restored*, a history of the Church in the latter-days. Judge A. Saxey, an officer in the Union army is quoted in his description of Missouri during the Civil War. The author, Carter Grant, was apparently quoting a book of memoirs. Why don't you look into that and see if there is a copy obtainable?

Not much of interest has happened this week. We watched a member couple have a fight, were given the "X" by a few of our investigators, and someone stole the mud flap off my bike. Pretty dull. . .

Love, Rod

All of us made use of German words even when speaking English, partly for convenience, partly for fun, largely because we couldn't remember the correct English word. The resulting broken speech was easy to follow, but a little more difficult when written down. The following letters suggest that the elders in Germany took it to another level.

6 *März* 1970, Rendsburg

Howdy,

Just written to say *Aufwiedersehen*. They (the mission president and the missionary committee) are sendin me to Salt Lake City for a complete physical examination. I don't want to go but I haven't too much say in the matter. The reason their *schicken* me back is *wegen* my lungs. The pain in them since I've been here has been about 50x as bad as it was when we were in the LTM. So they are going to try and find out what is wrong with the old *Körper*. After they find out what is wrong, if they do, I still don't know what they will do. Well, that's about it. Hope you'r doing better than I am. And remember: It is easy to approximate exactness, but it is hard to get an exact approximation. *Aufwiedersehen.*

Vieln' Glück. Bro. Welker

10 March 1970, Hamburg

How's the work coming in Austria? I hope you're doing better than me. I'm working hard, but no expected baptisms. I just got word Br. Welker is getting sent to Salt Lake for a complete physical. Br. Patten is in Berlin doing ok, and a couple of guys in our group baptized—Legler, Burnett, Grossnickle. I'll have to get on the ball I guess.

I got a hold of a great *Wohnung*. No shower, no hot water, the john is downstairs without heat and without a light. But I'm used to it. We've given some cool school *Vortrags*. Right now, I'm *freuen* myself *auf* spring.

Br. Hirst

13 March 1970, Wels

Dear Mom & Dad,

. . . Br. Schurtleff, the new DL, is introducing a number of "new" teaching techniques. They really aren't new, amounting simply to a series of questions designed to stimulate thinking. . . deep and challenging questions, and not answering them. This forces the investigator to think and to use his own resources; we help with that by talking about the *Book of Mormon* and prayer. . .

Last Sunday we had the Linz District Winter Conference, so got to go in and hear Pres. Broberg and others talk. It was really terrific! We also had a great snowball fight with the kids of the Linz *Gemeinde* (in suits yet!). Two sisters were baptized that afternoon too, which was inspiring.

One of our good brethren from the LTM, Br. Welker, North German Mission, is being sent home this week. He had had trouble with his lungs in Provo, and evidently they really became worse. So the Mission President ordered him home to Salt Lake City for a complete physical exam. He is a terrific fellow with an excellent knowledge of German. It looks like he will probably be sent to a warmer climate.

. . . I really appreciate all you have done for me and want you to know I really love you. It's wonderful that we are now united in the Gospel. There is nothing as important as that, and I rejoice in the day that we'll be able to all go together to the temple and share in that wonderful experience for eternity. . .

Love, Rod

15 March 1970, Wels

We four missionaries fasted and blessed the city from a hill in Thalheim on the other side of the Traun river. It had been raining, but stopped for our little ceremony. There is a high tower on the hill, but it had no lighting and is locked at night, so we just did it in a little wood alcove on the crest of the hill. It was cold as we bore testimony to each other. Bruder Fagar's testimony was particularly moving. We then all four said prayers in turn. Afterwards we had dinner at our apartment.

On 18 March 1970 Prince Sihanouk was ousted as the ruler of Cambodia. He allied himself with the communist Khmer Rouge in hopes they could restore him to power. Instead they, under the dictatorship of Pol Pot, seized control and ruled the country ruthlessly, forcing city dwellers to the country to work on farms and executing the resistant or putting them in concentration camps to be "re-educated". Two million people eventually died there amid scenes of incredible suffering. When President Nixon ordered military strikes against the Cambodian communists to suppress the aid and sanctuary they were giving the communist Vietnamese, he was met with widespread protest and complaint from the press, Congress, and the universities.

Chapter 7

20 March 1970, Wels

Dear Dad,

Happy Birthday! . . . I appreciate all you've done for me, Father. You have been for me a real example of Manhood (or, the Gentleman spoken of by Pres. McKay). Your patriotism, thirst for knowledge, love of beauty, and respect for mankind are all traits I'll cherish my entire life. . . (And) you've added to these many traits that of being a Man of God, bearing His Holy Priesthood. This will bring you and our entire family great happiness in the years to come.

I know that the Gospel is true and that we are engaged in the very real work of the Lord. I could never have received this testimony except for the background I received at home, where the love of you and Mother always abounds. And so, at this birthday celebration, let me say "thanks" to my earthly parents, the two most wonderful people I know.

Love, Rod

20 March 1970, Wels

Dear Mom & Dad,

Schwester Reisenbichler has taken a six week trip to *Düsseldorf* to visit her daughter, so we have the whole *Wohnung* to ourselves to take care of. That's rather exciting. Dear old Schwester Kapp comes over every day to clean and checkup on us.

We ate at the latter's yesterday—noodle soup, noodle and potato casserole, and salad—excellent! She's an interesting little lady and in great pain because of her gallbladder. She had her teeth knocked out by a drunk gypsy guard in a prison camp, had typhoid fever, and nearly starved, but is afraid of a gallstone operation because it's "worse than anything I've ever had to live through". These wonderful members here do so much for us; we really love them. . .

Love, Rod

27 *Maerz* 1970, Wels

Dear Mom & Dad,

From the lack of mail the past two weeks, I guess the mail strike in New York is having an effect. . .

Sunday we gave a special program to the branch to get them enthused about missionary work again. It seems to have come off rather well, so maybe we'll overcome the effect of two years with no baptism. We're being well received by people now, since we blessed the city two weeks ago. Many more people are listening to us. As we respond with increased effort, we are confident that increased success in terms of baptism and teaching will result.

Wednesday the rest of the district came in for a work-day in Wels. It proved most successful, findings at least 4 golden-looking people in our half of the city. In the afternoon of that day I worked with a Br. Metzner, a German missionary from Stuttgart. He was interesting to work with, and we had quite a good afternoon, finding among others an archaeologist, now studying psychology. We talked for some while, in which he showed us a number of specimens he had dug up. He also gave me a bag full of stuff, all found in Wels, dating from about 200 A.D. I'll be sending these on to you (Roman nails, pottery shards, etc.) . .

Love, Rod

2 April 1970, Wels

The work is advancing rather well. Many of our contacts are turning into investigators and making wonderful strides toward baptism. One woman, Frau *Swoboda, strikes me as particularly promising. The other day we challenged her to pray and told her she is eternal. At the end, when I said the prayer, she was in tears.*

3 April 1970, Portland

Dearest One—

. . . We went down to the plant and painted with Wayne last night. Now I find I have some muscles I wasn't aware of before! The plant is really coming along—Wayne is really doing a grand job, and he's interested in the whole thing. Dad is down there most nights. Katherine is filling out and is a very pretty little baby and a good baby. JoElle accepts her very well too, which helps. I'm doing all the washing, and boy that is a job. . .

(For Dad's birthday) Edward and Lynn called. They sent him a lovely book on *This Beautiful Land,* all about the U.S. It is a wonderful land and I sure hope it isn't lost because of all the stupidity in the higher offices. . .

Mom

3 April 1970, Wels

Dear Mom & Dad,

Wels enjoyed a white Easter this year. Yes, it snowed, pro-
digiously (and there is snow on the ground now). This, despite the
niceness of the weather lately. It's crazy, but then, we're a lot further north here than in Portland. . .

Our branch here in Wels has about 10-12 active members.
We meet in a little white building rented from a lady not having
any particular love for Mormons, but loving money more. Every
Sunday the missionaries (usually Sr. Reisenbichler, but she is still
in Germany) go in at 8:00 to build a fire in the coal oven so we can
have Sunday School at 9:00. Br. Eidherr, our Branch leader, gives
the adult Sunday School lesson while the children (both of them)
go downstairs in the basement for theirs. They don't have regular
bread for Sacrament , but use a *Semmel* for it (a hard crusted roll).
Lately we have been without a piano player, so Sr. Rudolph has
played her recorder flute as accompaniment. The sister who formerly played piano lives in Bad Ischl, which is quite a way away,
and due to winter weather hasn't been able to come. Shortly after
Sunday School the priesthood bearers meet in the basement for
Priesthood Meeting, three elders and four missionaries. We take
turns leading and presenting the lessons. They are two years behind in their lesson material for Priesthood class. At Sacrament
Meeting (6:00 pm) the priesthood bearers take turns speaking and
twice a month we have a speaker come to us from Linz. This
works out pretty well, each missionary speaking about once a
month. . . .

Love, Rod

8 April 1970, Portland

Dearest Rod,

. . . Edward leaves tomorrow morning! Do keep in touch with him while he's on his tour Dear. He really likes to hear from you—he mentioned it several times while we were there. . . Also keep him uppermost in your prayers. . .

Mom

17 April 1970, Wels

Dear Mom & Dad,

Tuesday I had a bit of a sore throat, so rather than tempt fate we stayed in bed and studied. Br. Fagar was down two months for going back to work too soon. I'm fine now, though, and we will probably be doing a little work tomorrow.

Br. Fagar was transferred this week to Wien. His replacement is a piano player, so our church music should be improving soon. Sunday we have Branch Conference and will be having Sacrament Meeting in Linz (Wels is a "dependent" branch of Linz). Also, on Tuesday we'll have an interview conference in Linz when we get our bi-monthly interviews with Pres. Broberg.

Today I prepared a box to send home. So far it's got my books (Grillparzer, Goethe, myths, plays), Roman artifacts of the 2nd century, a Christmas sock, some German pamphlets, and a calendar for Dad in it. . . . I finally got around to writing Prof. Tolkien last week—'will tell you when I get a reply.

Apollo 13 sounds in a bad way. We've been getting pretty

good coverage here, though it gets sort of garbled.

About one and a half weeks ago I worked in Linz with Br. McOmber and saw the Danube for the first time. It isn't really very blue, but beautiful just the same, winding its way through the city with the castle overlooking it (the castle at Linz does not at all resemble a castle). As usual, no pictures.

Though we have no chocolate chip cookies here (they sure would taste good if somebody would happen to send a "care package" full of them), we manage pretty well, with bananas from Africa, raisins from Crete, oranges from Israel (Jaffa, no less, where Grandma was born), tuna fish from Japan, chocolate from Switzerland, hardtack from Sweden, honey from Hungary, grapes from Yugoslavia, and peaches (canned) from California. And loads and loads of everything from Austria.

Coal is delivered in a large wagon drawn by two huge draft horses. The team is generally run by a dirty, little, old gypsy woman with no teeth. Something else we see often are old men walking down the streets pulling little wooden carts, gathering wood and junk. The wood I see use for, but 'darned if I know what they do with the junk. Another interesting sight are the chimney sweeps. One doesn't see many of them back home. . . .

Love, Rod

24 April 1970, *Wien*

Dear Bros. Duke and Saxey,

Howdy Boys! A lot sure has happened since I saw you all last. I rode into *Wien* with Br. Joes who climbed on the train in Linz. We had a good time, I'll tell you. I got to see Br. Archibald and Br. Mauchley the same day. Old Arch was carrying his old guitaree and wearing that old trunk out crust of his when I saw him in the Bahnhof. We met Br. Marv Wilkinson & Co. about 2 hrs. later. I'll tell you, working with this guy is really a crack-up. The first day he about "Pollack joked" me under the table.

We have been doing all right. The first door we hit we gave away a B of M and (taught) a second! My throat is still bugging me, but I hit my 4th doctor here in Beautiful *Wien* so things should be looking up. I may not get better, but things should be looking up. We might go see the opera "Macbeth" with an American member at the *StaatsTheater* for 60 cents apiece, not bad. Veradee (Verdi) wrote it so it can't be too bad. It premiered here about a week ago. Hey I sure hope you are doing as great as ever! I hope you are still smiling. May the Lord bless you always,

Br. Fager

25 April 1970, Linz

Liebe Brüder!

How's it coming guys? Man we hope everything's burning down there. We are expecting to baptize because of our labors in our area!! We think the West Zone is soo neat!! We really do have the best elders down here. We've also noticed how good you two get along down there in Wels!! We are always thinking about you and want the Lord's work to move forward, just as you do. To do that we have to follow the handbook. With the muscles you've got, Br. Saxey, it should be a breeze. With wishes and love we pray that you'll have a very successful week.

F.E. Waddoups, Jeff Larson

I often referred to being at the "Gates of Mordor"—Austria was on the border of the Iron Curtain, with the communists in charge just across the border in Hungary. Vienna was a center for espionage and intrigue not just in the early days of *The Third Man*, but throughout the Cold War.

The Austrian Mission had responsibility for Hungary and Czechoslovakia as well as Austria and a little corner of Germany, though we had no missionaries in those Eastern Block countries. From time to time the mission president or a visiting general authority would cross over to visit the few members who lived there and to maintain contacts with authorities in hopes of loosening restrictions. Missionary folklore led to rumor about the prospects for a few elders being sent in to proselyte. Always it was "maybe next year." It wasn't until the waning days of the Cold War when the Iron Curtain fell that those rumors finally came true.

27 *Aprile* 1970, *Milano*

Dear Brother Rod,

From your letter is sounds like the choice land of Austria is beginning to open up, and I just know the Lord's choicest blessings are awaiting the faithful who labor there. . .

I received a letter from Elder Lionel Nebeker who is in Berlin. The work is going great there, in fact, he and his companion had just been blessed with the baptisms of a wonderful woman and three of her children. The husband will follow, and two more children when they reach the age of 8.

Italy is booming! 115+ baptisms so far this year and the

momentum in the mission is growing all the time. *Milano* is having difficulty, but we're going to be baptizing soon. . . . My companion will be going home in less than two weeks—he's trunky & doesn't like to work! Though bad to say, I will be happy to have a new companion. . . .

The news about the East Europe countries—Czechoslovakia and Hungary—is truly exciting. Yes, my fingers are crossed! What an opportunity that would be! Go Austria!! . . .

What's the communist situation is Austria? It's really bad here in Italy. They grow stronger daily. Last Friday they held a 30 minute "power" parade through *Milano* by where we streetboard (set up a poster display to engage pedestrians in discussion). The streets were packed with students. The week before we had been forced to stop streetboarding when police teargas drifted onto the area from a very serious riot between communists and anti-communists. It's really getting bad. . .

May the Lord be with you in all you do. . .

Bro. John (Smurthwaite)

Communists and other socialists of various stripes celebrated Lenin's 100th birthday on 22 April 1970. In the United States they created the first "Earth Day." The celebration is credited to Democrat Senator Gaylord Nelson, who was rapidly followed by other lovers of big government (Paul Kengor, "Happy Earth Day and Lenin Day", *The American Spectator* online, 22 April 2013). They initiated regulations and created agencies to enforce them that would make any socialist proud. Even at the time the coincidence of the dates attracted attention. Kengor cites a Time magazine article dated 4 May 1970 that said, "It had aspects of a secular, almost pagan holiday—a sense of propitiating an earth increasingly incapable of forgiving what man has inflicted upon it."

The article went on to note that 100,000 marched on the first Earth Day in New York City, where the Communist Party USA and the Daily Worker newspaper were headquartered. "The Vietnam War was in full swing," writes Kengor, "and so were the war protesters, many of them peace-loving liberals who were easily duped by pro-Vietcong communist ringleaders like Mark Rudd, Tom Hayden, Bill Ayers, and Bernadine Dohrn (to name just a few)—who today (2013) are professors . . .

"Communists specialized in agitation and propaganda. They had a campaign for everything. They excelled at suckering impressionable liberal/progressive dupes, especially youth, whom they targeted at World Youth Festivals and via other deceptive activities. At this point, April 1970, they were having wild success with college students. Many of the major anti-war protests had communist fingerprints all over them. The documents have been declassified. . . Congress knew about the communist involvement and held extensive hearings. . . ."

The irony is unavoidable, for "if you want to see real pollution, the communist world had it by the river-load. It was horrid—toxic. If you want to clean up your environment, you need capitalism, because wealthy countries (which are free-market based) can afford it. When you're communist and dirt poor, your concern is bread or rice, not 'paper or plastic'." The irony continues: after presiding over the defeat of soviet communism by Ronald Reagan and Margaret Thatcher, the last of the USSR's tyrants, Mikhail Gorbachev, turned his energies and stolen money to building an "environmental organization", the Green Cross International, very much like the earlier Communist Party International which preceded it.

But I am getting ahead of myself. We missionaries knew nothing of such things in 1970. If we heard of "Earth Day" it was as a headline that we passed on the newsstand on our way to a day of tracting and I, for one, would have thought, "Just another dumb hippie thing." As for the environment, there was no litter in Austria, no garbage that we ever saw except in garbage cans; people just kept things clean because that is what civilized people do, and Austrians are civilized. Even a place that is rundown and old in Austria usually looks quaint and charming rather than just a dump. I suppose living in the same place for thousands of years requires clean habits.

24 April 1970, Wels

Dear Mom & Dad,

Chemtron sounds like a booming little enterprise. The house plants sound like blooming little enterprises too.

I received a reply to my letter to Prof. Tolkien. Unfortunately, though not unexpectedly, the letter was from the press offices of his publishing house. It was nice, though. I think I will send a postcard next time I'm transferred. . . .

Monday we had an excellent interview conference. Pres. Broberg was very inspiring. He is a terrific fellow and it's a pleasure to be able to work with him. Afterwards the 4 of us from Wels went to a restaurant near the train station for *cordon bleu* and ice cream. The president and his two assistants were there too, just across from us.

About a week ago we met family Hofmann. As you know, we send letters of introduction to families with new babies. This was one of those; somehow, however, they never received the letter. We approached them on the door and, being very interested to find out what was in the letter they never got, they invited us back. We gave a "Golden First" discussion. The man particularly is great. He gave straight "*Herr Braun*" answers for the whole discussion: I couldn't believe it. I thought we were back practicing with one of the listeners in the LTM. He accepted a baptismal date and a challenge to read, and he even reacted not unfavorably to the prayer and church attendance challenges!

The weather has been quite nice here of late. Last night at about 8:30 we went down to the train station to do a little tracting and it was about 65 degrees. Today it has rained and is about 60— a lot better than freezing!

I have developed quite a taste for yogurt lately. They have some really good ones, particularly cherry. I had stayed away from yogurt for quite a while due to the unfortunate flavor of a "*fru-fru*" I had tried.

I wish I could tell you half of what I have seen and heard and felt and done in the past seven months, but I have neither the time nor the ability. I have felt as never before the love of my family and friends, the fellowship and brotherhood of my co-workers, the respect and honor of strangers, and the hatred and envy of those who ignorantly choose to be enemies. (Most of the older people are fairly tolerable in this respect. It's the kids that make faces and call names that are aggravating. We have been making progress in that regard, however; Br. Duke's frisbee has "put us in good" with some of the little beggars.) All in all, the fleetingness of it all is most distressing. I shall often regret the fading of memory. . . .

Love, Rod

27 April 1970, Wels

Bruder Fager was transferred two weeks ago to Vienna. Old Tex had been very ill—was in bed nearly two months—but was improving. . . . The last day was hard on him. We had steaks that night, but he lay down, weak from exhaustion, preparing for the trip. Later he joined the party and he and I told the joke about Furries. Duke and I received a letter from him: he and Bruder Wilkinson are co-juniors and doing well; they taught a 2nd discussion on their first door.

Bruder Duke and I are getting along well. I like him a lot. He seems very close to the Lord. Bruder Shurtleff is improving with time too—he said at his last interview with me that he is "repenting."

I was sick in bed for about a week with a sore throat. We all feel the need of carefulness now, due to the great deal of sickness in the mission. At one point, every companionship in the country was out of action because one or both were ill. . . .

Still no baptisms in Wels. We have talked to a great many wonderful people, though. Just now we are teaching a Familie Hoffmann. *Last week we gave them a golden first discussion. It was beautiful, with a very positive response to a baptismal date of 16 May. We are quite hopeful about them, also some others, notably the Mehlführers. They are an engaged pair, the man a student in Graz, the woman a student of English attending Linz. We gave them a golden second discussion the same night that we heard the Chinese had launched a heavy satellite; that means they have ICBM capabilities. The news set a somber tone for the discussion. I said that this news intensifies the importance of our message, to which they agreed.*

Many of the problems we had in the Gemeinde *appear to be resolving themselves. . . Bruder Darhuber was sick a few weeks ago and I anointed him with oil and Bruder Eidherr pronounced the blessing. Schwester Dürnberger, upon whom Bruder Fagar and I performed a blessing some while ago (she was in a* Sterbezimmer—*"dying room"—at the time) should be leaving the hospital shortly.*

Last week we had an interview conference in Linz. President Broberg scolded us pretty well. Evidently there has been a lot of complaining in the mission, which is rebellion. He certainly put the complainers in their places. I love President Broberg—our little talk together really helped me feel right with all.

It is hard to believe I have been on my mission seven months already; it is also hard to think there has ever been a time I was not on a mission. Results? I don't know. I hope it looks better in the Eternal Spectrum of things than it does in the weekly reports. Our personalities seem to come with us from the Pre-existence. We go through cycles of trial and experience, then find ourselves pretty much where we started—changed, to be sure, and with broadened understanding we hope, but basically the same people we were before.

28 April 1970, Wels

Today was a flop as far as missionary work goes. In the morning we were at the church with the other brethren, cleaning out a corner full of junk. We ended up more wasting time than using it, which was aggravating. For lunch we had Schweinsgulasch *and* Palatschinken *for dessert, which was very good. In the after-*

*noon we talked to a few people, meeting a pharmacist who had
once lived in New Jersey. . .*

In the United States, the big news of the last weeks of April
were announcements by President Nixon of American and South
Vietnamese forces fighting in Cambodia against the North Vietnamese and their communist allies there. This was an important
part of the administration's strategy for an American exit from the
war, making South Vietnam safe from attack across the Cambodian border. The political and social climate in America was not receptive to the news, however, and there were many protests around
the country.

1 *Mai* 1970, Wels

Dear Mom & Dad,

I am experiencing my first May Day in Europe. We are also
having a cold wave and it has been snow flurrying all day. That
toned down the celebrations a little. At about 9:00 am a little group
of people led by a loud drum marched down the street alerting the
people that the time of the parade was nigh. We went down to the
town square where people were gathering. Banners and flags were
everywhere, some wrapped up in knots due to the wind. A large
stand was built in the square for the speakers. The people paraded
in (no floats or anything, just people marching around). It is pro-
foundly political, left wing, and is to demonstrate power. The socialists control the government now in Austria, so are particularly
happy this year. The communists were distinguished by the red
carnations they wore. There were lots of bands, clubs, and so forth.
Old veterans wore their medals. It kept snowing, so when the

marching ended and the speeches began, the crowd became quickly depopulated. . . .

I really like Wels and working with Br. Duke. It is probably the nicest town around, but must admit I am looking forward to being transferred in the near future. It is good to start over from time to time. . . .

'Bye, Rod

4 May 1970, Wels

. . . While tracting today we found a group of "sämtliche alte verrückte Weiben." I introduced us through the door to one lady, but she didn't understand and called another. I repeated. So did they. Before long there was a whirring chatter on the other side of the door, none of it understandable. ("What dog? I didn't see a dog. Did you see a dog?") Finally a younger woman—their keeper, no doubt—came and said through the door that they didn't want any. Bruder Duke almost lost it on that one.

On 4 May 1970 there was a shooting at Kent State University, Ohio, resulting in four dead and nine wounded. National Guardsmen had been called in to control demonstrations which had progressed to the riot stage; as can happen too easily in such tense situations, someone lost control. Colleges across the country closed down in protest. I did not hear details about this until after I was home, but talking about university protests in general, Brother Duke described lingering clouds of teargas in the air at UC Berkeley when he was there before his mission. He had to adjust his path to class or to home in order to avoid them.

8 May 1970, Wels

Dear Mom & Dad,

Saturday we had a street meeting in Linz. We arrived at 10:30 for the 11:00 meeting, but most of the rest of the brethren were there about 11:15. We started about 11:30 despite a cold wind and a drizzling rain. A group of 9-10 elders sang around a display board about the Book of Mormon while 2-3 of us passed out tracts. (My nose was stuffed up, so I was a tract-passer-outer.) At first they sang hymns, but there was no interest in it, so they started singing Negro spirituals. Not only was that more fun for us, but the people responded much better too. After lunch, Br. Duke and I stopped in at Linz Cathedral to look at the beautiful artwork—gold and fine woodwork. When we got back to the site of the meeting, though no one else was there. We looked around, couldn't find anyone, so went back to Wels. Later we found out they called off the meeting due to the weather. That was not a good idea, since the afternoon turned out nice.

It looks like our president is taking a strong stand in SE Asia. Not knowing any facts of the matter I can't say if that is good or bad, but at least it's better than the usual endless stream of meaningless words and rhetoric which have flowed from the White House in years past. The Austrians seem to hang quite heavily on what is printed in the press. Unfortunately, the press here is one of the most contemptible examples of "yellow journalism" I have ever seen. Emphasis is on sensationalism and debauchery. Huge headlines about "aggressive actions", "invasion", and "interventions" by the U.S. are all over the place. This will no doubt add to the anti-American feeling we encounter. One of the many problems we find is getting people to forget World War II—not a conversation goes by in which it isn't mentioned—and think about the good things of life which are, have been, and can be. All this nonsense in the news doesn't help our problem.

We have been having a series of special district study classes on the first principles and ordinances. The first week I gave a presentation on faith. I said essentially that faith is part of growing chain of confidence: hope, belief, faith, knowledge, certain or perfect knowledge. We move along this line of increasing confidence by a series of experiences which reinforce it. Hope is the wish (Alma 32) which we have that something is, such as that the church is true. Hope becomes belief as we give ear to the words and testimonies of others, placing confidence in them. Belief becomes faith the first time we act on our belief, such as decide to pray about the Church. Knowledge is a kind of faith which has been strengthened by many spiritual experiences or by one which was very powerful (the "burning" sensation in answer to prayer). Perfect knowledge occurs when we "see with our own eyes and hear with our own ears". When God himself tells us it is true and He reveals Himself. At that point our confidence is perfect, for we walk in the light of absolute knowledge. I went on to describe individual steps we can take in building our faith. . . .

Love, Rod

11 *maggio* 1970, *Taranto*

Dear Rod

Ciao!! . . .

I spent 6 months in Catania, a city of about 350,000 inhabitants located on the eastern coast of Sicily, and sits below the famous, still active volcano, Mt. Etna. I grew to love the members very much down there, and when I was transferred, it was sad to leave them. There were about 30 active members there, probably a few more. I am in the city of Taranto now, which is located in southern Italy just about at the "heel of the boot." There are over 70 members here, though not all active, and have found them to be very wonderful people also. . . . I suppose that the Church is a bit better established in Austria. . . I have had the joy of seeing 14 of my investigators enter the waters of baptism. Right now I am serving as 2nd counselor in the Branch, the Pres and 1st counselor being Italians. . . .

Every now and then discouragement sets in, but the work of the Lord will go forth, and He will sustain us in our low moments, if we will persevere and work with all of our faculties for Him. I am getting to the point where I am really enjoying and loving the work. We have a great bunch of missionaries here in *Taranto*—8 elders, 3 sisters, and an older couple. Every Sunday night we hold Family Home Evening at the couple's apt. It is really special and gives a big boost to our spirits every week. Last night we were a bit late in getting started, so we just sang together for quite a while, and then we feasted on two giant, homemade banana cream pies! To our dismay we learned that the couple is being transferred to Rome. We will miss them greatly. . . .

Your brother, Phil (Stark)

Later, when we were all back together at BYU, Phil remarked how marvelous it was to walk along the harbor and hear fisherman or dockhands singing opera as they went about their work. It was the perfect place to send a musician. He and John were also among those recruited to perform in a series of "missionary concerts" as a special assignment while they were in Italy.

As for Edward, Lynn's work as a stewardess for TWA made it possible for them to rendezvous at various exotic locations around the world, which was a great boost to their morale. His work aboard the USS America proved at times tedious. Visits with Lynn were, I am sure, much more enjoyable than the long distance chess game we tried to carry on from time to time by mail, one move at a time.

The *America* had been built in the early 1960s and entered service in 1965, had homeport at Norfolk, Virginia, and was usually assigned to the Mediterranean. In 1970 she was on the line in the Gulf of Tonkin, flying over 10,000 sorties without a loss due to combat, including the first combat flights of the A-6C "Intruder" and A-7E "Corsair II" aircraft. The new aircraft gained headlines, but Edward's F4 remained the workhorse of American airpower. The published histories say there was only one major accident in that deployment, and that with no fatalities. Edward's letters indicate the experience was not quite so rosy.

11 May 1970, Honolulu

Dear Rod,

'Enjoyed your letter so much. It came after Ed left, so I took it to Rio for him to read & he really enjoyed it too. He will write you soon, but if you haven't heard from him yet just be patient as his mail service is rotten! It should improve once they get over to the East, but now, especially during this 3 weeks from Rio to the Philippines nothing will be going off or on the ship. It's as hard on them as us.

I am now flying international flights again . . . 'Hope to have a trip into Hong Kong when Ed is there. . . . Lynn

12 May 1970, Portland

Dearest Rod,

. . . Randy Rowley got his call Friday to Japan. He graduates from High School on the 6th and must be in Salt Lake on the 7th. He's so excited. . . .

14 May 1970, Portland

Dearest One,

. . . You mentioned the mess the dear US is in. Boy! We went past State College on Broadway last Saturday before the cops moved in—it was so disgusting and—can you imagine chairs, boxes, rags, etc., piled up about 7 feet on all the streets bordering the school. All the lovely park blocks—all these stringy, long-haired, dirty characters standing there waving their arms and shouting, giving the "peace" sign with one arm and the "Black Power" sign with the other.

Dad went down and watched from a distance when the police moved in. There were 32 treated for injuries in all. Those dirty so & so's throwing rocks and spitting on the police until they got the word to move in. It makes me so sick I'd like to cry over the conditions of this beautiful land of ours. And our generation was the cause of all this permissiveness in the youth of today. The young folks the ages from yours to Edward's—I thank God each day that our three boys turned out so well. We tried to do right by you boys. I can say my heart bleeds for the parents of these youth, but some (so many) don't even care, I'm sure—God pity them!

. . . We are so proud of you . . . Mom

14 May 1970, Berlin

Dear Rod,

. . . Our work here is going forth, but not as fast as I would like to see it. It seems we talk to more *Ausländer* than other people or regular Germans. We are really finding our greatest success here by working with the members. We can find people and teach them, but it is the influence of God and association with the members that brings them in. May the Lord bless you and your companion with Success!

Love, Don (Waddell)

14 May 1970, Wels

Today was most interesting, full of little surprises of all sorts. In the morning we went to Schwester Rotheneder's for breakfast. We were invited by letter in a rather secretive fashion because of the problems with gossip in the branch in the past, notably at last Christmas when the missionaries last ate there. We had hardboiled eggs and cold bacon—it was excellent! The breakfast was also in celebration of my birthday, which is next week, so a cake was there too. Schwester R gave me a book of sayings and proverbs we had both looked at during the party at Christmas. It was really very kind of her.

In the afternoon we did a little tracting, but finding it unfruitful, decided to go over to the other two brethren and check out plans for tomorrow (we are going to help Bruder Eidherr work on his country house). We then went to Schwester Eidherr to certify arrangements and visit. By that time it was almost time to eat something (we had skipped lunch), so we went down to the Gasthaus zur Österreichischen Hof, which the missionaries called "Rusty's" because of the shade of red stone the building was made of. The Gasthaus part was closed, so we went into the adjacent cafe and ordered something to drink. We were then informed we could not get food at that time, so we decided to hurry with the drinks so we could go to the Wienerwald.

The waitress was a young blonde who speaks "du-Sprache" with every male who comes in. At the time she was talking to a disreputable looking fellow near the cash register. About the time I finished my drink they got up from their table and went behind the counter of the cafe. I was looking at our newly received catalog of mission supplies and did not notice the couple's actions until I heard a loud thump and some scuffling. Looking up, I could see the top of the fellow's head over the counter. I feared that he may have knocked her down and be trying to rob her (I heard change clank onto the floor).

I looked at Bruder Duke, but he did not know what to do, not having been paying attention. I stood up quickly to ascertain the situation. The woman, hearing my noise, got up (Bruder Duke said she was putting on her skirt) and started shuffling things about on the counter. The man remained kneeling behind the counter. She was quite red and would not look into our eyes. We paid, left, and, finding the owner of the place in the adjoining Gasthaus, told him something was out of order in the cafe. He went to check it out and shortly came back. He said only the waitress was there, he asked her what had happened, and she would not speak. He apparently knew things like this happened and was quite put out by it. He said all the young women are whores these days and apologized.

Morality is in such a degraded state that it is not uncommon for missionaries to encounter prostitutes, but it is rare for us to interrupt them in the act. Of course, few would practice their profession behind counters in public cafes, even if the only other patrons present are two green Mormon missionaries from America.

15 May 1970, South and West of Indonesia

Dear Ricky,

Since leaving Rio we haven't received any mail nor has any left the ship. The closest we've come to land is when we came within 10 nautical miles of Cape Town, South Africa. . . . We haven't really been into our cruise very long now and already have had several changes to our itinerary and probably can expect many more before we are through. . . .

How about starting up our chess game again? . . . Edward

16 *Mai* 1970, Wels

Dear Mom & Dad,

. . . Yesterday we went to Br. Eidherr's new house and worked for the day. He's building a house in the country, about 15 km away in Eggendorff, and has to tear down the old one first. We took a bus there, through beautiful country exactly like home with hills and trees, the only real difference being the *Bauernhöfe*, large farm houses with home storage, and barn all under one roof around a central courtyard. Many are hundreds of years old. We worked from about 7:00 until 2:30, tearing down walls, stacking bricks and lumber, and playing with Br. Duke's frisbee. For lunch Sis. Eidherr had *Knödel* with an excellent mushroom sauce. When we got home we went to the town sauna (we were really tired and dirty) and lounged for a couple hours, then all came over to our house for scrambled eggs and cheese.

I received your letter today telling of Randy Rowley's call to Japan. That is really exciting! I heard a rumor that the traditional European mission countries would shortly and gradually be reduced and that that force would be re-directed into the Far East, where the work is moving forward more rapidly.

. . . According to letters received by Br. Duke from Berkeley (where he attended last year), U.S. campuses are in turmoil—except for BYU's. If you happen to see a good article, send it. Our news reporting here is unreliable. By the way, we met a fellow the other day who actually likes Americans, not with the fawning money-hungry "like" we sometimes encounter, but just earnest friendliness. Missionaries tend to get a skewed view of things because we come in contact with so many kooks and wise-guys. . .

Love, Rod

18 May 1970, Wels

        . . .

Today was Pfingsten (Pentacost) and therefore the tracting was not too good. We did meet one rather interesting fellow though. He is the 82 year old head of a large auto repair firm here and calls himself an "old soldier" and an "old Austrian". What's more, he is. He told us of his experiences and honors and accomplishments. He taught the last emperor how to drive; was decorated three times on the front, once by the emperor himself; fought on all fronts (World War I, of course; he was not much of a "Hitler-

mann") excepting the French and one other; and rose in the ranks from corporal to some sort of important commander. . . When we met him, he seemed as spry as a man of 50.

Because we grew up hearing stories about World War II, our generation tends to forget the dramatic disruption of the European social order that occurred in World War I. It was not so much a prelude to the second war, as the second was the conclusion of the first. This was particularly wrenching for the Austro-Hungarian Empire, which was broken into pieces, many of which had been together since Charlemagne. The adversaries in 1917 had fought each other to a standstill and were exhausted in every sense of the word: the stage was set for reasonable compromises and a peace treaty that might have been kept. Then the "progressive" president, Woodrow Wilson, broke his promise to "keep us out of war" and launched a crusade to "make the world safe for democracy." Thousands of lives later he got the unconditional surrender he required, but democracy was not safe for long.

20 May 1970, Wels

Well, here I am in the last day of my twentieth year and I am sick! It all started yesterday with a queasy feeling. We knocked off work and I went to bed about 4 pm. By evening I had a fever of 101.5. Between the heat and the uncomfortable bed, I could not stand to stay down, so about 11:30 got up and read in Job for an hour. The fever had plateaued, but by morning had come down to 99.6 and by noon was normal. I feel weak, dizzy, and have headaches when standing, but am otherwise normal. Schwester Reisenbichler was in a tizzy about my sickness. She gave me a shredded apple as medicine, but with instructions not to eat any-thing else—I was hungry, though, and upset her by having some soup.

I am overcome with joy as I consider the blessings of the Lord. My parents are now fully active members of His church, the family of my father has prospered and enlarged, and I am able to serve God in this beautiful land. I am so very grateful for His great goodness and mercy.

20 May 1970, Wels

Dear Mom & Dad,

Our district is planning a bicycle trip to *Kremsmünster* next Friday, so I thought I would write tonight while I have time. Yesterday I was sick and ran a fever through the night. It broke this morning and we're taking it easy and all's well. Tomorrow we are invited to lunch at Sr. Rotheneder's again.

Pres. Rector, one of the 7 presidents of the 70, comes next Wednesday to hold interviews. I am expecting a transfer soon also; President Broberg said he doesn't like leaving someone more than six months in one place. Don Waddell wrote that all is well with them—it is great to hear word from other corners of the Vineyard.

The more I see of the world, the more I appreciate the wonderful home life which you have given me. I am ever and again impressed by the words of the patriarch when he said, "you have been carefully shielded and protected from the forces of evil." The thought of home and dearly beloved family remains a constant source of comfort and joy. . . .

Love, Rod

26 May 1970, Portland

. . . Our dear country is really in a terrible state, and I'm afraid it's going to get a lot worse before it ever will get better. Our national leaders need all our prayers as does the country. . . .

Mom

28 May 1970, Wels

Dear Mom & Dad,

We decided to take our free day Thursday and try to shake our sore throats by staying home. We both feel better and think this will work. . . .

I spoke again last Sunday in church. We have been averaging once a month speaking, but I managed to get in twice this month. . . . As usual, I talked overtime. . . .

Love, Rod

22 May 1970, Wels

Yesterday I ceased to be a teenager. In the morning we went to Schwester Rotheneder's for a discussion-lesson about the Sunday school lessons (she teaches the Junior Sunday School, so can't be in the adult class). Afterwards she gave us a lunch of spiced venison with a dessert of chocolate and ice cream—it was terrific! In the afternoon we picked up Schwester Kapp at the Bahnhof and escorted her home. She then gave us a snack of home-made Leberwurst and Russischer Kraut. The kraut wasn't bad, but the Wurst smelled like the viscera of a sheep freshly butchered. I almost could not down it, especially after so marvelous a lunch. I managed to cram it down though, and in the evening she made me a nut cake we will eat today. At Relief Society meeting that night Schwester Darhuber gave me the little bunch of flowers she had brought for the church.

Today we had planned an outing to Kremsmünster, but it is raining. When we went to the brethren in the morning to check on whether we were going they gave me a cake with 20 candles. That was really a surprise, and very nice of them. Schwester Kapp's nut cake was terrific. All in all, this was a very cakey birthday.

28 May 1970, Wels

Yesterday we had an interview conference in Linz. President Rector, one of the seven presidents of Seventy, interviewed us. He asked about my family, and I told him of my mother's conversion, which pleased him. He is a very dynamic and well-informed speaker. In the course of the day he indicated the time for dividing the "wheat from the tares" in the church is almost here, that the change to President Smith as prophet was smooth and good, and that changes were coming to the extent that in five years we would not recognize the various programs of the church. He also said there were a lot of threats against the church at the last conference. One crank phoned in a report of a bomb under the tabernacle. When Pres. Smith was told this he told them, "Nonsense. There is no bomb." The conference was held without disturbance.

In the evening he gave a special talk to the members in Linz and afterwards was asked to bless a sister with multiple sclerosis. I happened to be there, so wheeled the sister into a classroom where the ordinance was performed and was allowed to participate in the circle. Br. Larson anointed her and Pres. Rector pronounced a blessing with the greatest priesthood power I have ever heard. He blessed her with strength, promising she would walk again, and further blessed her that she would have her family in the church and live a fruitful life of service. The blessing was not given "according to your faith", but simply promised.

The expected transfer arrived the next day.

Chapter 8

I had grown to love Wels and felt a distinct sense of loss as the farms and villages of *Oberösterreich* flew past the train window. I feared that I would never see those dear people again. Gradually the plain gave way to hills, then mountains, and sorrow was replaced with excitement as I approached Salzburg.

If Vienna is the mind of Austria, then Salzburg is its heart. It is a maze of streets and alleys lined with wonderful buildings demonstrating great architecture from many periods, with the beautiful cathedral and the *Residenz* palace of the archbishops at its center. From the *Pferdeschwemme*, an exquisitely carved and ornamented fountain for bathing and watering horses, to the magical *Mirabell* garden on the other side of the river, from the *Festspielhaus* for plays to the *Mozarteum* for concerts, the city is filled with art and music. Towering above it all is the *Festung*, the fortress never conquered, that was emblematic of the archbishops' power.

In one of the many city squares, not far from Mozart's birthplace, is a fine statue of the composer. When excavating to erect the statue a Roman plaque was found, on which was inscribed in Latin, *"Hic habitat felix"*-*"Hier wohnt das Glück"*, or in English, *"Here dwells happiness."* It is an appropriate motto.

Salzburg is built along a bend in the river between mountain ranges of Bavaria to the north and the *Salzkammergut* to the south. The trade in salt from the mines in the *Salzkammergut* was a major source of the city's wealth. To the east are the hills and plains which lead to Linz and to Wels and further to Vienna. To the west is the *Untersberg*, a majestic elongated mountain beneath whose peak Kaiser Karl (Charlemagne) is said to slumber, surrounded by his knights in a large cavern. It is also said that when the empire is in greatest peril, he and his knights will awaken and ride forth to the rescue. To the best of my knowledge they have not stirred.

Bad Reichenhall is just over the border into Germany, a health resort that grew up around hot mineral springs in a small valley between towering mountains, opening toward Austria. I am not sure if there are any more picturesque places in the world. Erich Kästner wrote a sweet little novel titled *Der Kleine Grenzverkehr* (*The Little Border Traffic*) about a North German attending the Salzburg Festival during the thirties when they were only allowed to take a few marks out of the country at a time; so he rented a room in Bad Reichenhall and every day had to travel back and forth to Salzburg with only a little change for coffee, but charm enough for romance. With church, district meetings, and other duties in the city, we would now experience our own *kleine Grenzverkehr*.

31 May 1970, Bad Reichenhall

We received our transfer in the regular mail on the 29th. Luckily we were at the other brethren's when they received a copy or we would not have known about it until the afternoon. I am here with Br. Graham as co-seniors to open the town to missionary work; the last missionaries left here about nine months ago. We have no tracts, copies of the Book of Mormon, *or any other supplies. The apartment is really nice though, and the area is beautiful. We arrived in Salzburg yesterday; that is also where we will be attending church. . . . we expect to see much success.*

Today we dashed all over the place to get everything set up so we can work. We talked to a good member we have up here, Bruder Schubert—he is very sharp, young, and vigorous.

1 June 1970, Bad Reichenhall

Dear Mom & Dad,

. . . This is one of three or four German towns in the Austrian Mission. I arrived in Salzburg at 5:00 pm, Saturday. The DL took us and part of our luggage to our apartment here that night. They picked us up the next morning for Priesthood Meeting in Salzburg. In the evening we drove our bikes back through a driving rain—oh, the joy! We find we have to take a complex series of bus and train connections to go to Salzburg (where we attend church and missionary meetings) . . .

Things are more expensive here. The room costs about $17-18 (not sure exactly—60 DM). Meals in Wels were about 85 cents, here about $1-1.50. Then too, I have to buy new shoes (a second pair, that is), white shirts (the old ones are falling apart), socks, and a new suit one of these days. I can get a really good suit of *Trevira* for about $25 through a big order house here. I think it will work out alright, though, without dipping too far into the emergency fund, so don't worry.

It is really beautiful here—the first three days it rained—with mountains all around except for a large pass in the southeast towards Salzburg. The town is about 14,000 in population and has no industry except tourism. . . . The Romans had a bath here. Baths, health food shops, drugstores, camera shops, and tourist junk places are all over, ready to suck the poor, dumb, gullible tourist for all he's worth. A roll of film that costs $2 in Salzburg, also a tourist destination, costs $4 here.

We're starting pretty much from scratc. There is one good member family, a few old investigators, no supplies, and incomplete area reports. It makes life interesting. Br. Graham is interesting too, from Tampa, FL. His German is a little hard to understand, largely due to his Southern accent. That makes for a rather different situation from Wels—Br. Duke spoke practically as good a German as I do. . .

Our *Wohnung* here is pretty nice. The beds are even flat and give evenly when you press on them! We are in the third floor, with two windows, and access to a little kitchen in the balcony. The *Hausfrau* is just starting to realize Mormons aren't an order of Catholics. As a matter of fact, she may even come so far as to realize we are not even *Evangelisch oder Lutheraner*. . .

Love, Rod

Brother Graham proved to be a great companion, a tall, skinny guy with prematurely graying hair, sincere eyes, a deep voice, and a great sense of humor. I referred to his accent as Floridian, but he was actually quite proud of the fact that he was born and raised in Charleston, South Carolina, and his accent was from there.

8 June 1970, Bad Reichenhall

The work here is progressing slowly. We are both convinced we will baptize here and are working hard to see it. This is an incredibly beautiful place with mountains all around. Sunday we took the train to Freilassing, then the bus to Salzburg. At the border the bus emptied and everyone walked through a pass check, re-boarded the bus, and shortly thereafter changed buses for the rest of the trip.

Today we talked to an old investigator. He is a leading teacher here, but does not believe in God, saying he is not capable of it. He said I spoke like a lawyer, defending the faith, which made me feel good as far as my German goes. The week before leaving Wels I gave a talk in church that approached what we would call in English a sermon and apparently it had a good affect on the members.

It was kind of hard to work with Br. Graham at first. He was the D.L.'s companion and feels a need to lead. I suppose that made us even. We have talked about it and now that we have seen each other in action, we are adjusting. He is a very good missionary and we will be able to work well with each other.

9 June 1970, Bad Reichenhall

Tonight we visited the Schuberts and had a nice conversation. He explained to us how the German system of insurance and health resorts works. Most people come to Reichenhall on "Kur". They are sent by their doctors with expenses paid by the state through their national insurance. He explained that the term "Bad" meant that the town had passed certain regulations and tests to qualify as an especially good bathing and health resort area, a spa. The traditional fame of this town is in the salt water springs (Reichenhall means "rich in salt"). In the Kurgarten, the large park in the center of town, is a large building covering a stack of sticks over which the salt water flows. This causes a salt spray which is said to be healthful especially for bronchitis patients.

Bruder Schubert told us of a trip he made four years ago to Greece and Crete and even showed us a film of it. It was really grand and further whetted my appetite to make the same trip. His best friend, Herr Wiegand was present, who was his companion in Greece. Herr W. had been an investigator, but now claims to be an atheist. The evening seems to have strengthened our feeling with both the Schuberts and Herr Wiegand.

Bruder Schubert commented that I don't look American, but German. Then he added, "like a Catholic priest". I mentioned that I've been told that before a lot, except before it was always more particular: "an Austrian Catholic priest"! He turned red and said that was exactly what he had thought, but didn't want to say it. This is the same comment I have heard from many others, notably Schwester Rotheneder in Wels, and this time I did not even have my Catholic-looking suit and sweater on.

10 June 1970, Wels

Howdy Sam!

Guess what—my new comp got sick (with angina) and we have to stay in for three days. Br. Shurtleff, Br. Reed, and Br. Harris all have the same bug, so the whole district is pretty much immobilized. I hope your detachment is not suffering so badly.

We managed to contact Herr Wist and we're going to give him your address—he wants to write you! We went back on Hauer and his wife said she thought he'd read the whole B of M! He still wasn't too friendly on the door, though, and one appointment fell through. We'll go back though. He has TB and has lost a lot of weight; evidently he's had it for many years. We talked to Hofmann, too, and he took a liking to Br. Summers (they are both mountain climbers).

The other brethren are looking for a new *Wohnung*—their *Hausfrau* is getting too much for them to take. We made contact with a neat lady (friend of Schw. Rotheneder) who worked for 2 years in the LDS Hosital in Salt Lake. The big problem is that she is a widow with two kids, who is messing around with an older man with a reputation as a "Don Juan". She may make it, though, if we can get her trust.

My new comp is really interesting. Former SDS (Students for a Democratic Society, a communist front organization) president at Utah State U. and "politically" very radical (Revolution!) Egad! We manage to get along great, though. He's got some fantastic missionary talents—people automatically like him. And he knows how to make pizza, too. He's even got Schw. Reisenbichler in the best mood I've seen her in. She laughs and jokes with us all the time now. Who can figure it?

I managed to get a wedding invitation from an old girl-friend this week, too. Things aren't dull, but I still miss my good ol' sidekick, Sam. You take care of yourself and really show those old orcs what a fight we Hobbits can put up.

May the hair on your toes. . . . Frodo

p.s. We're on foot again. Br. Summers has a hernia. And I discovered today that my bike was stolen out of the cellar. Like I said, life isn't dull!

12 June 1970, Bad Reichenhall

Dear Mom & Dad,

I am standing in a radio shop while Br. Graham plays a letter tape (his recorder is in repair). The past few days have been hot—20-23 degrees C—then yesterday it started raining hard, harder than I have ever seen it rain before. Today it is hot again.

We only have one member here, the Schubert Family. They are really great people. He is in the Salzburg Branch presidency. . . .

We gave a strong faith and prayer lesson the other night to *Familie* Bock. They are an old and good investigator family with intellectual testimonies, but who won't pray (the wife will, and does, but the man is stubborn). We fasted and prayed about them and feel the pair will be baptized; it will take a while though.

Another investigator we're working with is a woman of about 30 with 4-5 adopted children. She responded beautifully to both the 1st and 2nd contacts, volunteered to come to church, and told her son, "You want to go to church and hear about Jesus, don't you? Be good now. God sent these men to us to teach us." Wow! We told our DL about her and he said the last time he heard that was from a family in Wien. They're members now. . . .

I thought red tape and bureaucracy were bad in Austria, but Germany is worse. The other day we got three packages of supplies from *Wien*. The official wouldn't believe that a *Book of Mormon* only costs 2 DM and pamphlets nothing. Anyway, after a long form, an hour of bickering, and a trip to the apartment to get our copy of the order, we finally got off with only paying about a dollar. A similar situation was when we registered our presence here. We had to fill out a form twice as long as the one in Austria and the official gave us another three page form for visas. Now, you don't have to get a visa until after three months, so he's trying to scam us. We won't go back until we have to. . . . Rod

14 June 1970, Innsbruck

Today we had a marvelous conference in Innsbruck. The rented bus of the Salzburg Branch picked us up at 12 at the Bahnhof (it was supposed to be at 11:30, but Mormon Time seems to be universal). We arrived in Innsbruck at about 2:30. In the afternoon a couple of the brethren went into town and got a bucket of Speck's fried chicken, which we ate on the lawn. We then took a trolley into town and looked around the "old town". That evening the Salzburgers presented a roadshow to inspire enthusiasm for the upcoming productions. They did a spoof of American commercials—it was hilarious.

The night was spent in a youth hostel—pretty grimy and crumby, but tolerable. I met a bearded young man from California who has been bumming through Europe since October. He spent about two weeks on Crete (I gotta' go, I gotta' go).

Our meetings were great today. Two of our investigators, the Bocks, attended the main session. After Sacrament Meeting Jackie Scott, a member of my BYU "family", came up and said hello. She is here with two friends travelling Europe. This is the third time I have met people from home. The first time was Dr. Owings, one of Dad's employers; the second time was last week, when in church there was an old school chum of Dad's, escorting his son home from the North German Mission. In the afternoon we drove back to Salzburg.

Many of the shop people here know a little English. They often assume we are tourists and try to help us by speaking English, but our German is usually a lot better than their English and it can be annoying when they use it, sometimes without noticing that we are not. The other day day I took in some shirts to be cleaned and the woman said, "to press 'em?" To which I replied, "Wie, bitte?" "Press 'em?" "Wie, bitte?" "Zum bügeln?" "Ja, bitte schön."

19 June 1970, Bad Reichenhall

We walked into a most interesting situation last night tracting. The first house we knocked at brought us a man who invited us to come in and take part in a meeting which had just begun. It turned out to be a group of about 18 "Free Christians", or something like that. They opened with songs and about half an hour of praying in turn. Their prayers became quite wild to the point of a semi-trance. One woman even gave forth to be speaking for God in the first person, prophesying. When the prayer was over the preacher got up and gave a sermon about unity and love. It was largely a good talk. I could not resist such an opportunity to address a group, so when he finished, I asked if I may introduce us. I told them we appreciated their earnest seeking after truth and that they were being prepared for the gospel. No sooner had I mentioned Joseph Smith than the preacher curtly interrupted me. He then offered a closing prayer in which he gave thanks that we do not need prophets nowadays like they did before Christ and expressed gratitude at being able to keep false doctrines out of his congregation. Immediately after the prayer he unleashed a tirade against us, Joseph Smith, and the Mormons in general. Before we could reply, he dismissed the group. Afterwards he said such blatant lies to us personally as I had never heard before, so we testified briefly and left. (At least one family that was there subsequently let us in to teach the Joseph Smith story because they felt sorry for the preacher's treatment of us.)

Felix Nestlinger was one of the great landmarks of the church in Salzburg, a delightful man with a kindly, honest spirit, short of stature, but big of heart, and well known throughout the city and surrounding towns. In 1927 there was a pair of new missionaries whose German was not understandable. An investigator knew that Nestlinger spoke English, so called upon him to translate for him. As he did so the message of the Gospel sank into his soul and he was converted. In January 1928 he was baptized, the same year the branch in Salzburg was first organized. Among his kindly deeds was his famous car tour of the *Salzkammergut*.

19 June 1970, Bad Reichenhall

Today Br. Nestlinger took us on his tour of the Salzkammergut, the rich mountain region around Salzburg. It was overcast, but picture-postcard beautiful. We saw Mondsee, Gmunden, Attarsee, Bad Ischl, Bad Aussee, Hallstatt, and more. Br. Nestlinger is an authentic, old-fashioned, hand-kissing Austrian who always wears Trachten, the traditional grey Austrian costume with bone buttons and green trim. Everyone knows him. He gives a "cuckoo" call when he arrives and everyone leans out of the shops and waves. The swans on the lakes are his special friends and they come when he calls them; "Hansi" he calls.

In Gmunden are ceramic bells which play a Schubert melody each hour. There is also a castle on an island in the lake (named Lake Villichee by the Romans) which was originally built by a ghost as a wedding requirement for an elvish maiden whom he loved. In Hallstatt there isn't room to bury everyone, so every few years they dig up the bones, clean them, and pile them by type.

In the "bone house" are over 2,000 skulls, neatly stacked. In the church at St. Wolfgang is an immensely valuable altar which was almost thrown away by a short-sighted priest in the 15th century. Also in St. Wolfgang is the "Inn of the White Horse", about which a famous musical was written. The last emperor, Franz Joseph, had his summer residence in Bad Ischl, which was also the birthplace of Franz Lehar, the composer. It was a great trip and we thoroughly enjoyed it.

19 June 1970, Bad Reichenhall

Dear Mom & Dad,

. . . We are working with some great people now. They are making progress toward baptism, too. Please pray for them. They are Frau Stark and *Familie* Bock. They are really great people and if things go right I should be able to tell you about at least one baptism in a couple weeks. Frau Stark is the one who told her son, "God sent these men to us to teach us." She is golden—we gave her a golden First with "Br. Braun answers" all the way. We challenged her to be baptized on July 3rd and, come to find out, that "happens" to be her birthday. Due to relatives we are going to have trouble meeting with her. . .

Last Saturday we went to Innsbruck with the Salzburg Branch for District Conference. We didn't have anything to do until evening, so looked around the town. It is very beautiful. . . . Monday we have to go to Berchtesgaden for visas. We had wanted to go to site-see, but Pres. Broberg said we couldn't. Now the Germans are making us go for official reasons, so . . .

Love, Rod

Berchtesgaden is a beautiful little alpine town filled with picturesque views and lovely old buildings, many with murals that add to the natural color of the locale. Alas, its greatest fame is as Hitler's favorite resort, "The Eagles' Nest". We did not have time to tour, but the name brought to mind Professor Hugh Nibley's description of being the first Americans to arrive there and finding cups of coffee still warm on the table and cigarette smoke still lingering in the air. Nibley had served a mission in Bavaria in the late twenties and used to speak of the discouragement he felt. Later, as a soldier working for Intelligence ("Order of Battle", which often meant he was out in front, reporting his observations) he visited many of those same towns and villages. He remarked in his lectures at BYU how much easier it was to go door to door with an M1 carbine than with a *Book of Mormon*.

19 June 1970, *Wien*

Dear Sax,

I understand that you're in one of the most beautiful cities in the mission with one of the greatest missionaries on the range—I'm glad to hear it.

I got a letter from Br. Olsen (Dan) from up in *Deutschland* and found that Br. Charles Olsen and Morgen are seniors. Muhlestein was senior at 3 months. Bro. Dixon and McDonald are doing great. Bro. Anderson is in Berlin. Bro. Bates is tearing up the South & I'm supposed to tell you all Hi!! from Teddy.

This Wilkinson cat is really a crack up. It gets awfully deep around here sometimes. We have shovel shifts.

We talked to a genuine Russian hardline "commie" the other day and the only thing that I can say about their system is "dumm". He isn't happy. He told us Russia would take over the world—a Kruschev diehard. I told him to study up on Mormonism after he thought there was a 10% chance of a God existing. Then I told him he better watch Mormonism "real close" because that's where he and his system are going to really bounce off, crash, and burn. The Russian Embassy is in our area and they, the Russians, are as easy to spot as missionaries. I'm turning into an Ezra Taft John Bircher.

The work is going great. We're talking to guys from Greece, Mexico, Malaysia, Belgium, Scotland, and all over.

Tell Bro. Graham Hi and big bussies (little forward ain't I?) Thanks for writing Br. Saxey. Keep Smiling & don't spend too much time leaning on your shovel.

Sincerely, Your loving Bro. Fager

24 June 1970, Bad Reichenhall

Since challenging her to baptism it has been nigh unto impossible to contact Frau Stark. Today we managed to teach her a second discussion, but halfway through some old Hausfrau came in, a typically obnoxious Frau X type, and started talking, so we will have to come back and try again. She is really golden, but we may have trouble making the date.

We had to move downstairs from our very comfortable apartment to cramped quarters on the ground floor. The toilet is outside and around the corner, a smelly little stool in the corner of a large room without running water (we have to flush with a bucket) and without a light. There is no bolt for the door. (I think the Hausfrau figured out who we are.) At least they provide toilet paper. That is better than the places where they use newspapers.

On 24 June the United States Senate repealed the Gulf of Tonkin Resolution. Shortly thereafter the South Vietnamese took over the border defenses which Americans had previously held.

26 June 1970, Bad Reichenhall

Dear Mom & Dad,

. . . And now for the medical news: Br. Graham has tonsillitis, which has infected his nose, eyes, and throat. We therefore took him to a nose, eyes, and throat doctor, under whose care he is doing better. The pain from my hemorrhoids finally became more than I could take, so I went to a doctor and got $5 worth of suppositories, salve, laxative, and bath preparation. It all seems to be helping, though I can't sit in one spot very long. . .

We're taking two baths per week now. The heat has been pretty bad lately. Every night, though, there is a thunderstorm. That's grand; I love storms at night. . . .

Love, Rod

3 July 1970, Bad Reichenhall

Dear Mom & Dad,

Well, that July 3rd baptism isn't coming through. Stark's husband had been talking to the neighbors, who filled him full of garbage about the Mormons. He thereupon forbade our coming in the house or that she go to church. She wants to come and be taught "on the sly", but of course that doesn't go. She's the most golden investigator I've seen and would be baptized tomorrow if we told her to, she trusts us so much. We'll talk to the fellow Saturday and try to settle his fears.

We fasted with Sr. Bock yesterday that Br. Bock may admit the truthfulness of the Gospel and be baptized, and that Herr Stark may be affected to let his wife be baptized. Sr. Bock is really golden, and br. Bock believes it's true, too. He was taken in, deceived, and disappointed first by Nazism, by the Catholic Church, and then by the Jehovah's Witnesses. He fears committing himself and being disappointed again. They are really great people, though, and like the missionaries, and will be baptized soon. Tonight we're going over to give a special lesson on the blessings of baptism.

This town is great and we've been talking to a lot of people. If we are "fishers of men", then "the fish are biting!" I'm sure we will see some real success here.

Last Sunday in Salzburg we went to a cafe and had cheeseburgers with fries, and ice cream for dessert. It wasn't too bad, though not quite what we wanted. Afterwards we went park tracting down by the river. I got to talking to one fellow who turned out to be a tramp, and invited him to church. He said he would come sometime and then tried to pan-handle me, so I told him I would give him five schils (20 cents) if he came to church. That night he came and tried to pan-handle a couple of the leading brethren (on the excuse he had to get back to the hostel by 8:00 and needed a ride or money). Anyway, we funneled him over to Br. Nestlinger, who told him it wasn't true about the hostel—they all close at 10:30. That scared him, meeting resistance. Br. N gave him 5 schils to ease the pain and he disappeared. "That's all he really wanted anyway," he said.

The weather has been dismal, rainy all week. We make quite a pair, riding down the street, steering with one hand and holding an umbrella in the other. Also, last Sunday they had a wedding. It was a little odd; after the Branch President married the couple, he spent 5-10 minutes bearing his testimony and giving a big plug for the missionary work. I've heard of Missionary-Sacrament Meetings, but Missionary-Weddings?

I bought a second pair of shoes the other day for about $10. They are pretty nice. Just wearing the one pair wasn't too good. . .

Love, Rod

3 *Juli* 1970, Wels

Hi Sam!

How are things in Bad Reichenhall? . . . Br. Shurtleff is in the hospital, recovering from a tonsillectomy. Their new *Wohnung* is in the middle of the city. Sis. Reisenbichler still spits in the sink. . .

May the Lord bless your efforts, Sam, and grant you happiness. . .

Love, Frodo

10 July 1970, Bad Reichenhall

Friday we gave the Bocks a special lesson on baptism. She became excited and on Sunday was all set to go to church. He said no, though, which deflated her. He then went onto the balcony and lit a cigarette, something he never does at home because she objects. This really ticked her so she went storming onto the balcony, took the thing out of his mouth, and tore it up! This from one of the meekest, most retiring souls we have met. Later on he suggested they go for a ride in the mountain. She said, "If you won't go with me to church, I won't go with you to the mountains." Wow! Twice in one day.

Tuesday I broke my tooth on the crust of a piece of buttermilk bread, so Thursday we went to Salzburg early to have my broken tooth fixed. Br. Grünauer, the only Mormon dentist in Austria, rebuilt it in about 15 minutes for free. We had a couple hours on our hands, so went to the Residence Palace of the Arch-bishops, who ruled Salzburg and the surrounding region for centuries. The art exhibit was fantastic—mostly from the 16th-18th centuries, including works by Rubens, Michelangelo, and Rembrandt.

We went down to the church later and found a young man sitting on the steps. He and his friend just got out of high school and are touring Europe; they wanted to see if they could stay with a member family. One of them, named Rapp, is a non-member, so we taught him about Joseph Smith, the Book of Mormon, *and the Plan of Salvation. He is very sharp and receptive. In the evening I spoke at a baptismal service about the Holy Ghost.*

We have overcome the Mann-Problem with Stark (he agreed to let us teach her), but now cannot get in to talk with her. For the past week we have tried every day to get in to teach a third discussion, but for one reason or another have been unable to do so. We don't know what's going to happen with her.

10 July 1970, Bad Reichenhall

Dear Mom & Dad,

. . . We are talking to a lot of really sharp people now. One school teacher we have was astounded as he saw our filmstrip about archaeological evidence for the *Book of Mormon*.

Thursday we took a strawberry cake to Sr. Bock for her birthday. We had tried to do it the night before, but were caught in a thunderstorm and soaked.

They divided our district, formerly the largest in Austria. We are now in Saalzach District, named for a river here, and it is composed of us, the brethren in Braunau, and two brethren in Salzburg.

We are on a careful budget—eating at home and avoiding little expenses here and there, so next month should prove better than the last. . . .

Love, Rod

On one occasion when we were visiting with Br. and Sis. Bock, the topic of World War II came up. They were sweethearts at the time; Br. Bock had been an enthusiastic member of the *Hitler Jugend* and wanted to join the SS. She begged him not to, so he relented and simply served as a regular soldier. Then her eyes filled with tears as she told how they noticed foul odors coming from the concentration camp outside of town. After the war the Allies made them tour the camp and they learned about the Jews being killed there. "The soap we used, was made from their bodies," she said, her face filled with revulsion. "We didn't know."

11 July 1970, *Wien*

Hi Sax Babe!

It is hotter than ever here in *Wien*. Today is Bro. Wilkinson's birthday and we are sitting at the *Wienerwald* for dinner. Yesterday we went with Bro. Feil and comp to *Schönbrunn* and ate a quart of ice cream each. I got a letter from Br. Welker—he got a medical release on the 23rd of June so now he's taking summer school at the "Y" and dating like crazy. Big Dan Olsen told me to tell you Hi. My Dad and Mom and Family went through the temple and boy, am I happy. Tell Graham howdy and write, ok?

Tex (Br. Fager)

It might have been easy to assume a Mormon cowboy from Idaho had been raised in the Church, but life has a way of surprising us. In the meantime my own family back home was progressing toward the temple too.

14 July 1970, Portland

Dearest One,

. . . Sunday evening we went to the Woods' for the evening service (Temple Preparation Class). It's supposed to last one hour, starting at 7—we didn't leave until 10:30. Everyone had questions, and of course, Don Wood is a terrific talker anyway. . . .

Mom

17 July 1970, Portland

Dearest One,

Enclosed is a card from a young fellow who talked at our meeting Tuesday night at the Stake House—Joachim Pestinger. He was in Wels a couple of years ago on his mission. He had 3 baptisms while there—maybe you have heard his name. . . .

I finished reading the *Book of Mormon* yesterday. It's an amazing book. I wish I had read it before going to Mexico. We'll all have to go two years from now. I think we'd all enjoy this. In the meantime read the book again and then really go there with the intent of tying things together in our minds. . . . Mom

17 July 1970, Bad Reichenhall

Sr. Stark accepted a golden third discussion and lived the Word of Wisdom for at least a little while. Her husband then forbade her going to church and told us not to come back. We will let him cool off and try to reason with him.

Sunday at church the Pony Pipers, a group from Milwaukie Oregon, sang. In the afternoon Br. Graham and I went to Renate Duchet's to talk and eat a snack. She is very nice, suffering from some sort of paralysis that keeps her confined to a wheelchair. She is very sweet, about 22 years old, with long dark hair, and worrisome. After church she said to me, "I like you." That she is cute and intelligent contributes to the worrisomness of the comment. She will be in Italy for three weeks, so I won't have to deal with it just yet.

Tuesday President Broberg was in Salzburg for interview conference. It was great to see him. . . . We taught the Schaefer family in Reichenhall-Türk a golden first discussion. Afterwards they fed us a dinner of Wurstls, little sausages. That was terrific, even though it made it so we did not get back to bed until midnight. They are a wonderful young family and we are quite hopeful for them.

17 *Juli* 1970, *Wien*

Dear Br. Saxey!

How are you and Br. Graham doing these days? Tell him Hello for me. That's pretty good, my two LTM companions working together. Things in *Wien* look real good right now—especially in the way of upcoming baptisms. Our best investigator is a young med. student, Br. Ebert. He's had 4 discussions and is challenged for July 25.

I was real happy to hear from you and that you like Bad Reichenhall so well. Keep up the good work and let's show these Austrians where the "in crowd" is. Hope to hear from you again real soon. *Seien Sie recht lieb gegrüsst (Br. Graham auch).* "Be right lovingly greeted (Br. Graham also)."

Br. Labrum

24 July 1970, Bad Reichenhall

Dear Mom & Dad,

. . . Being busy is the sure road to happiness. We see a lot of people who aren't busy and they are unhappy. One of the pat answers we get on the door is "No time." Now, it is true they work long hours over here (not hard, just long). When one pursues the matter more closely, however, one finds their free time a chaos of waste. Hours on end are spent gossiping, drinking in the inns (a national pastime, resulting in another national problem, the beer belly), and watching TV (it's worse here than in the U.S.). . .

Saturday the districts of Salzach and Salzburg went to the little town of *Braunau am Inn* for a work day. This is the town where Hitler was born. I saw the house, a plain building just like the one next to it. The door was unlocked, so we wandered around inside—nothing much to see. It's up for rent right now, without a sign to identify the place as that where one of the most infamous criminals in history came to earth. Interesting, that every store with a display of postcards had some cards with a picture of the house on them, also unidentified.

We had considerable success that day, talked to a lot of people. The next day Br. Behunin and I stayed for church. In Sacrament Meeting I was the main speaker and talked half an hour about being a Latter-day Saint. Then Br. Behunin sang a song, followed by a brief address by Elder Lundberg, who is Branch President. It was a great meeting and everything held together well.

The past two weeks have been a little slow. I have been taking daily sit-baths prescribed by the doctor, and Br. Graham has been taking it easy so as not to inflame his tonsils. He goes into the hospital on August 4th and remains until the 11th. I don't know what I am going to do during this time. I've been a loner my entire life, but since being here I've lost my companion a few times and it is frightening! I imaging Br. Behunin will have a tag-a-long in Salzburg for a few days. . . .

Br. Hartmann, an investigator, is making good progress. We introduced the Word of Wisdom the other day and he's working at it. He has troubles because of muddled thoughts and difficulty in concentration, but is a wonderful fellow and should make it.

We're talking with quite a few neat people just now. It's really exciting to tell people about the Restoration and see the Spirit bear testimony. I am glad to hear you read the *Book of Mormon*, Mother. It's a great book, and better than that, it's true.

Love, Rod

30 Juli 1970, Wels

Lieber Bruder Saxey!

. . . Vorige Woche wie Sie ja bestimmt wissen werden, ist Br. Duke versetzt nach Wien! Es hat mir sehr leid getan, wir haben uns noch näher kennengelernt, er ist wirklich ein lieber guter Jüngling, so wie Sie, lieber Br. Saxey!

Es ist schade, dass soviele Menschen nicht bereit sind, die Botschaft des wahren Evangeliums, anzuhören von den jungen Männern die der Herr aussendet!!! Ich bin bis an mein Lebensende und noch darüber hinaus dankbar, für die Gelegenheit, diese wahre Kirche kennen gelernt zu haben! . . .

Viele lieben Grüsse dazu, Ihre ergebene,

Sr. Rotheneder

von Sr. Kapp herzliche Grüsse.

(Dear Brother Saxey!

. . . As you certainly know, last week Br. Duke was transferred to Vienna! I was very sorry to see him go, for as we had gotten to know each other better I found him to be a dear young man like you, dear Br. Saxey!

It is a shame that so many people are not ready to listen to the message of the true gospel taught by the young men that the Lord sends!!! I will be grateful to the end of life and beyond for the opportunity to have learned about this true church! . . .

Many loving greetings, respectfully yours, Sr. Rotheneder

Sr. Kapp sends hearty greetings.)

31 July 1970, Bad Reichenhall

Generally speaking, this has been a pretty rotten month. Ever since the interview conference our hours and work quality have been poor, at times depressingly so. . . . At least part of it is the heat, and then too, what with the hot weather and all, we have had trouble with bikinis.

First there was Fräulein Brieschenk, a young lady about 18 years old who came to the door in a two-piece that seemed not to fit right. She would be a good contact, but unfortunately not the type we can work with just now. Then there was another woman on the top floor of a Stiege. Her child had told us to come back some other time, so we went down to the next floor. She then came to the banister, leaned over, and called us back. I backed up the steps and began a door approach and, as Br. Graham says, suddenly developed a "shocked" expression. There is nothing to take your mind off the work like a bathing suit that barely covers.

A couple weeks ago we were in Braunau am Inn. It is a little town and we ten missionaries accomplished a lot in a short time. . . . It was a pleasant day, especially travelling home in the darkening of the evening. The landscape reminded me of Tolkien's Shire, rolling countryside with many woods and well-tended farms and little towns built around churches on hills.

We found a place where we can get pizza.

31 July 1970, Bad Reichenhall

Dear Mom & Dad,

. . . Sunday I spoke in Sacrament Meeting in Salzburg for

18.5 minutes. That's pretty good for a 15 minute talk. Also Sunday we went to Family Hartmann's for lunch and had roast rabbit with giblet dressing. That was terrific. Br. Graham didn't like it much though, but he's a Floridian, so we can forgive him.

Monday I went to the doctor and he gave me some more stuff, including pain pills, thank goodness. It's taking so long to get rid of this problem and the pain is so bad at times I begin to wonder about this doctor. If something doesn't happen soon we'll be looking for a new one. Medicine is notoriously corrupt here and "doctors" are a dime a dozen. That's what socialized medicine does. . . .

Our landlady decided we were using too much electricity so had a meter put in our room and will be charging us for it next month. We will be looking for a new room anyway. . . . We made arrangements to talk to some youth groups and are looking forward to it.

Love, Rod

31 *Juli* 1970, Hamburg

Dear Rod,

It's really great to hear from you again and to see you're seeing success here in *Deutschland*. Your little health resort looks real cool. I'm only afraid that I'd go tract out the forest and mountains instead of the people all of the time. I must say it's been a long time since I've seen a "real mountain."

Well, I came here to Hamburg on the 21st of May and have been here now for 2 and a half months. During this time we have received a new mission president and I must say it is an experience that I hold as quite valuable. You can really tell what the elders really are by what they say and do. Also, we have some contacts here that are really great. I think they'll hit the water pretty quick. They are a result of member missionary work.

By the way, I think your mission president is good friends with ours. Maybe we ought to talk them into an exchange program so we could see and work with each other. But seriously, Rod, we are in the Lord's work and may He bless us both is my prayer.

Love, Don

3 August 1970, on Yankee Station

Hi Folks,

. . . Today is our last day of this line period. I have two hops, one over the beach and one forcecap. That will put me over 100 traps on the America, and 75 combat missions (counting last year). This has not been a very good line period for the Squadron in that we have had a lot of aircraft problems as well as the loss of our second airplane. The R/O made it out ok, but the pilot was killed. But after today we head for Hong Kong. . . .

The ship is going to spend 3-4 days in Subic and then 3-4 days in Manila Bay before leaving for the line again.

I'm enclosing a couple of photos that I thought you might like. Ted (my pilot) and I took pictures of each other on an alert-5 one day. And the other is with our Skipper when I pinned on my Lt. bars. That's right—made it effective the 1st day of July. . . .

Love, Edward

4 August 1970, Tokyo

Dear Rod,

Well, I have been out for two months now and I sure do love it. . . . It sure is nice here in Hawaii, so very beautiful and the people all are so full of love. I sure would like to stay here longer, but it's almost time to leave for Japan. Yesterday about 150 Japanese saints came over to do temple work and we got a chance to put our new language into effect. It was quite different and really difficult to communicate, but fun. I sure love those people. They just have something special about them, maybe because they are my people. We were able to go through the Hawaii Temple twice, once in English and once in Japanese. One learns so much in the House of the Lord, it never ceases to amaze me. . . . It sure is a joy to be in the service of my Father—I love Him so very much. I pray that He might give us strength to do whatever He may require of us. . . .

Elder Rowley

Randy Rowley was a member of our Priests' Quorum in the Portland 15th Ward, another of our number who were tutored, as it were, in the Gospel by President Wood and Bishop Waddell. Despite the challenge of a difficult language, his faithfulness and humility made him a fine missionary.

Chapter 9

7 August 1970, Salzburg

Br. Graham had his tonsils out two days ago, so I am working here in Salzburg with Br. Behunin and Koji. That is something else again, tracting with three instead of two. Instead of slamming the doors with a groan, the little old ladies slam with a scream. Br. G's operation was quite difficult and he is still very weak, I have had hemorrhoids for some while now and they have been painful, and Br. Koji hurt his ankle. Pres. Broberg is coming up today to talk to us.

Last night we three went to the Mozart Marionette Theater and saw "Die Entfürung aus dem Sarail", an opera by Mozart. These puppets are world famous and their fame is well-deserved. At one point while one of the figures "sang" a solo, a peacock "flew" across the rear of the stage, stopped, spread its tail, played around a little, then flew off again. It was an utterly fantastic and enchanting performance. . . .

Wednesday we went to Reichenhall to talk to people, among whom was a major in the German medical corps. We had tracted him out the week before and he told us to come to him in the Kaserne (barracks). We did so and gave him an excellent first discussion. At the gate we were stopped by guards with machine guns; under guard we went to the major's office—it was quite exciting. That evening we contacted an investigator here in Salzburg who is remarkably like Herr Wist. This one is a student of German history and well read in philosophy. We gave a fifth discussion and he accepted it very well, but, as with Herr Wist, refuses to pray.

Somehow the humility fails.

12 August 1970, Salzburg

Tomorrow I will be going back to Reichenhall to stay, as Graham comes out of the hospital. It will be good to be in our own area again. There is no substitute for the feeling of belonging. These brethren have some great contacts and investigators, though. Last Saturday we worked in Braunau; I was supposed to have stayed there for Sunday, but had forgotten my pain pills, so came back here instead.

I have felt down lately, I think because of that feeling of being out of place I mentioned above. Br. Behunin is an interesting fellow and a very dedicated missionary; he gets the job done well. Br. Koji is still very green, has a fear of speaking German, and seems to lose patience sometimes. But they are good brethren. One of their contacts is a Russian count. He is something of a professional investigator, but nice, and every bit a scholar and philosopher. He is quite well off, and gave the brethren a thousand schillings to buy tickets to "Jederman" for Saturday for the whole district. Strike one up for the Russian aristocracy!

14 August 1970, Bad Reichenhall

Dear Mom & Dad,

. . . Br. Graham came out of the hospital yesterday. He lost his tonsils, but still has his accent. Floridian isn't as bad as some other accents I can think of. . . .

Love, Rod

14 August 1970, Portland

Dearest One,

. . . Portland is surely going to be in a turmoil, what with 14,000 Legionnaires here for their convention, and over 20,000 here for the "Rock Festival" and the 15,000 due for the "Love Demonstration". Where will it all end? The county of Clackamas gave the "Rock Festival" permission to use McIvers Park, which is terrible--that's only about 4 or 5 miles due south of our place on the Clackamas River. . . .

Now the demonstrators demand the use of Washington Park and Delta Park—the city just spent $1,500,000 to build and seed a new golf course at Delta Park. . . . When these "pot smokers" move in they thoroughly strip and ruin the grounds they use. Can you imagine these two beautiful parks and also the others after this? They have cancelled all leave for police, National Guard, etc., so all of the Protectors will be on duty. This is all supposed to take place the week of August 24 thru to Labor Day. We are dreading it!

"Howdy" looks so grand this year. He has developed into a massive dog, "spitting image" of Old Topper! "Lekey" is developing into a lovely female even with the tear on the one ear. She's getting quite large now; she was born Jan 9th. . . .

Love you Dearly, Mom

18 August 1970, Bad Reichenhall

It is good to be with Br. Graham again. We have not done much yet, but have had some wonderful experiences nevertheless. On the 15th we went into Salzburg where we saw the famous play,

"Jederman". It was indeed a great performance, done in front of the cathedral. The plot is, appropriately enough, very Catholic, but touches on some important eternal truths, namely sin, repentance, forgiveness, and redemption. Br. G and I were distressed because Br. Behunin had not remembered to change some marks into schillings for us, so we were limited on what we could buy. Sunday we went to church in Salzburg where I saw Renate, recently returned from Italy.

After Sunday School we drove to Vienna for the All-Mission Conference. Brother Monson spoke that night in the Sacrament meeting in the Wien II Gemeindehaus. There were a great many present, including all the missionaries, a negro member family from France, and Br. Monson's beautiful 16 year old daughter. I saw all my old buddies there—Duke, Fager, E, Labrum, and all the rest. Br. E was in a bad way, though, with spirits down. We and Br. Duke talked and prayed together, but it did not seem to help much. Thank goodness he managed to have a word with the Apostle the next day. . . .

After the meeting we had lunch in the Relief Society room. We four dropped over to the mission home, which has been greatly improved through remodeling. On the trip home we stopped at a special place for banana splits. Today we were visited by Behunin and Koji—they are both being transferred. Oh Weh! I felt quite attached to Br. Behunin.

12 August 1970, Bad Reichenhall

Dear Mom & Dad,

. . . Tell Br. and Sis. Rudolph that I met Br. Schulz. He is a missionary here and a cousin of Sis. Rudolph. He's a pretty sharp fellow, going home this week, and said he wants to look you up, Mom. I'm not sure exactly where he heard about you, but he seemed pretty impressed. . . .

Sunday afternoon after Sunday School we drove with Behunin, the DL, to Vienna for our conference. After hearing Br. Monson speak at Sacrament Meeting we all went to a renovated castle used as a youth hostel where we tried to sleep on awful beds for the night. The hostel is co-ed, which proved distressing for the first elders to try to go into the washroom that night. In the morning we had a breakfast of hot *Semmels* with butter and jam and curdled milk (first they tried to give us coffee, then tea—poor cooks, they didn't know what to make of it). We had a great conference that day. Br. Monson spoke about the work and we found out that, statistically speaking, Austria isn't the slowest of the German-Italian missions after all—Switzerland is. We had a question-answer period. He indicated there is a good chance the rumors about thousands and thousands more missionaries being called may become true (I have heard the number of 40,000), but that "in the long pull" the number in Austria will average about 100, less than at present even. He concluded with an account of the calling and ordination of President Smith (the new prophet).

We fasted with Br. Schubert on Wednesday and gave a blessing to his wife that evening. They didn't tell us what her ailment is. Afterward we all had supper together. I've been able to give a number of sick blessings since being out. I told you about the first one, back in Wels with Br. Fagar. The woman was in the "dying room" and the doctors expected she wouldn't make it. About two Sundays before I was transferred she was back in church for the first time since the previous November.

We tried to teach Br. Hartmann last night, but he really

seems hopeless at times. He seems to totally lack any power of concentration and becomes terribly muddled in his thinking, but he wants to believe and to hear more, so we will go back. . . .

Love, Rod

26 August 1970, on Yankee Station

Dear Folks,

We really enjoyed our visit together in Hong Kong. Lynn got there in the afternoon of the 7th of August. The ship got in the morning of the 5th and that's the day I had the duty, so I didn't get off the ship that day, but the 6th I went ashore. You see, most of the time a large ship like an attack carrier has to anchor quite a way out. So we either use our own small boats to shuttle people to shore and back, or in the case of Hong Kong the ship hires small boats (called walla wallas) and some large ferries. . . .

The ship pulled out the 8th for a day and a half because of a typhoon . . . Edward

At this time Mom and Dad were preparing to go to the temple, not only to receive The Endowment, but also to be sealed together as husband and wife for eternity. The sealing ceremony is brief, but profound, elegant, and beautiful. Their civil wedding had been on 25 September, Dad's parents' anniversary. Despite their apparent down-to-earth practicality, the Saxeys turn out to be a family of real romantics as indicated in the following. Raile and Faye were Dad's older siblings, still living in Utah at the time.

26 August 1970, Portland

Dearest One,

'Got a letter from Mildred yesterday. She and Raile are going to the temple with us too. She told me when she was here in June that she really felt bad because he had never taken her and she said she thought that was her greatest desire, so when we decided to go I wrote them and asked if they would make Sept 25 a real family anniversary. After all, it was the folks' anniversary, also Faye and Forrest's, and ours, and now our temple one too. So after writing twice about it she wrote that Raile hadn't said a word until last Sunday when he went in for a long chat with the bishop and so now they are planning to go with us. She's so excited. . . .

Love, Mom

28 August 1970, Bad Reichenhall

Our new District Leader is . . . Br. Freckleton. His companion is Br. Allen, a really sharp young student of psychology who has already served in the army. Br. F. gave us the news that Br. E has been sent home. That is too bad, for he is a good man, but apparently the pressure was too much for him to take. That means that of the 18 who came out on the great "Big Ben" transfer of December 4th, only 16 are left. Br. K was sent to England after two months in hopes that a more familiar culture and language would make it easier for him, but has since been sent home after assaulting a woman at the door. Those who are left are Duke, Fager, Labrum, Graham, Nielson, Jones, Feil, Sheranian, Wilde, Ogilvie, R, Hicken, Wilkinson, Lowery, Arbon, and myself. All have spent time in Vienna except Graham, Nielson, Arbon, and me. Labrum has been in Vienna . . . and is now the Zone Leader's companion.

Last week while tracting we met a little old lady who invited us in. We tried to give a "first four" (the Joseph Smith story), but she did not show any interest. She then invited us to lunch Saturday. She was so confused and confusing, we did not know what was happening. We were to meet at the Bürgerbräu. *We half expected to be conned into buying her lunch, but when we went to pick her up she said she was sick—probably a way of chickening out. Saturday night we had branch Family Home Evening in Salzburg. It was pretty neat except they had a devil of a time making the projector work, so we ended up missing part of "The Windows of Heaven".* . . .

Monday we gave Brieschenk of bikini fame a fifth discussion. It was quite pleasant—she fed us ice cream and was moderately responsive to our message. We have been able to do a good deal of teaching lately. Tuesday night we ate at the Jägers' and had red chicken. They were embarrassed, but the hen really was done, despite the color. On the way home—it was rather late—we met Corey, a young member from Minnesota bumming across Europe. He had been in church in Salzburg Sunday and was now headed for Zürich. He was tired, cold, and hungry, and did not know where to stay for the night, so we invited him to stay with us. We fed him an Eintopf *(stew) and let him sleep on the floor. The next morning we let him sleep in while we went to Salzburg for study class. Erika, the landlady's daughter came in to clean and found him there. Later she said, "Ich war ganz erschrocken. Es war ein grosser, wilder Mann darinnen!" (I was completely shocked. It was a big wild man in there!)*

Thursday we had a work day with the new brethren. In the evening we went to Kittenbergers for Family Home Evening. It was really sharp—Sr. Kittenberger, Luise, Liselotte, a number of elders, investigators (Frau Horkel and sons), and other members for a total of about 15. It was enjoyable with lots of Küchen after. Also yesterday, while tracting, we met a woman from Walla-Walla, Washington. She is very nice, a singer at the Mozarteum. While tracting in another building a man became very angry with us. We had not spoken two sentences before he "Xed" us. As we were at other doors he came back out, became very angry, waved a shot-gun at us, and threw us out amid curses and oaths.

28 August 1970, Portland

Dearest One:

. . . Last Sunday was Brad's and Doug's farewell. Brad is a very good speaker. . . He'll be a good missionary I'm sure. . . .Plan on getting back for the Fall term, no matter what else comes or goes. . . . Keep praying for your brother Edward; his last letter says he'll be starting home in about 2 weeks, but the paper says the *USS America* is to stay in the war zone. . . .

Love, Mom

1 September 1970, Portland

Dearest One,

Today it is raining—everyone is happy (except the Hip-pies!! Ha!!) It's just a gentle one with temps in the high 60s or low 70s. Beautiful!! It's hard to believe that it's again Sept. You have been gone almost one year now and I was baptized almost a year ago. Granddad's been in Mexico almost a year. Time surely flies by. . . .

Edward's war cruise is over half gone now and God has been watching over him. I do pray he'll bring him home safely. Do pray with us on this. Also, do keep up your correspondence with him. He loves you very much and he needs you. . . .

Love, Mom

3 September 1970, Bad Reichenhall

Last Friday we blessed the city. Brüder Schubert, Jäger, Nikisch, and we fasted until about 4:00, then met at Schroffen, *a Gasthaus on the side of a hill not far from our apartment. We hiked about five minutes up the mountain to a secluded spot Br. Graham and I had found earlier, from which we could see the city. Br. G. conducted, Br. Nikisch opened with prayer, Br. Schubert testified of the priesthood, I spoke the blessing, and Br. Jäger closed with prayer. It was a very good little meeting.*

Saturday the branch had a pioneer celebration. It had been nice all day until evening, when it began to rain. The celebration therefore began in Br. Zechmann's home near Leopoldskrone's Moor. Leopoldskrone is where much of The Sound of Music *was filmed. Later in the evening, as the rain stopped, the party was transferred to a camp fire in a clearing in the moor. It was a neat party with songs and even a little square dancing (no, we did not take part in that, though we wanted to).*

The cute little blonde girl who has a crush on me was in charge of the money so she enjoyed asking for my ten schills. I was out of money, so sent her to Br. G. Sunday we visited Renate Duchet again. It was a nice way to spend the afternoon, except that she has a crush on me too. (Why can't this sort of thing happen when I am not on a mission?) Sunday night I was with Br. Freckleton while Graham was in Braunau giving a talk. We went to the Kittenberger's for supper; later in the evening Luise slipped and addressed me as Herr Saxey. Liselotte corrected her, but she blushed and whispered something to her, ". . . Renate . . ." Egad!

3 September 1970, Bad Reichenhall

Dear Mom & Dad,

. . . Saturday we gave a special Word of Wisdom lesson to Br. Hartmann. After a lot of urging, he accepted it. We poured out his bottle of beer, took away his cigarettes, and gave him candy and near-beer for substitutes. Monday when we went back he tried to get out of his commitments, but he knows what is right. He had had only one schnapps and three cigarettes over the weekend, which is real progress for him. . . .

We had an interesting meeting Tuesday. We showed a *Book of Mormon* filmstrip to Fr. Hofmann and her friend from Düsseldorf. They are descendants of old aristocracy and always talk like they have their noses in the air and everything. The aristocracy around here is fun to talk to, though it is usually hard to get them to humble themselves.

Saturday I told a Joseph Smith Story to a family from Munich in the park. Their son is living with a friend in Portland right now, so we had a good conversation about Oregon. He had written how dry it is there, and hot with no rain. How about that for Oregon?

Yesterday we had lots of fun riding home from one of our tracting areas, which is a few miles away. We took a neatly tended little road through the woods, a road just for pedestrians and bikes. It was nicely paved, running near the river for a long way, but then suddenly became a narrow path with bumps and mud. It was drizzling and the brush was soaked and soaking. Up and down, through the muck, over the rocks, around the trees, over the roots—it was the most fun we've had in a long time!

There are some advantages to having a companion from the South—new recipes. Today we had grits and bacon and eggs. One of our favorite meals is peas and rice. Good old Southern food. I can hardly wait for a chance to travel around the U.S. and see what there is to find. . . .

Take care, y'all, Rod

9 September 1970, Bad Reichenhall

The Schäffer family was in church Sunday and seemed pleased. During Sunday School song practice Sis. Schäffer leaned over to me and said, "But these are all happy songs!" "Yes, they are," I replied. They are very sharp people, but we have a hard time meeting with them because he works in Munich. . . .

It rains almost every day here in late summer. In the evening it clouds up and thunders. We have been soaked pretty often already. Two days ago on the way home from Br. Nickisch's in Marzall, I saw the most beautiful lightning I have ever seen. It was colored red and violet, silhouetted the mountains, and was at times jagged, linear, or in balls. This marvelous place seems unreal, like another world out of a Tolkien novel.

It was hot the other day when we visited Sr. Bock. On the spur of the moment we ran to the store down the street and bought three packages of ice cream and a lemonade. Sr. Bock was amazed. She said in an entire summer she does not eat that much ice cream. She did well, though, and downed a fair share. She was happy to have a break with us.

I had a very good discussion with Br. Schubert the other evening when we took shelter there from the rain. He is wonderful, with an excellent understanding of the gospel. . . He gave us each a book the other day. Mine is Brueder Im All, *about the likelihood of extra-terrestrial life. He is really sharp, hoping to go to the temple with his wife soon. . .*

I received today a most welcome letter from Edward, who is presently on the line in Vietnam. He included pictures. He is a Lieutenant now. As I read I began to feel how very much I appreciate my brothers. He said Duane Sparrow, Lynn's younger brother, died September 1st in a fireworks accident. . . .

3 September 1970, Portland

Dearest One,

Just a note to let you know Duane Sparrow (Lynn's younger brother) was killed Sept 1st. He and another boy were making a small bomb like you boys have done and it went off and killed him instantly. Oh, I feel so very sorry for them. This leaves them only Lynn and Edward. Do write them and also Lynn . . . We are driving up for the funeral tomorrow. . . . Mom

3 September 1970, on Yankee Station

Dear Ricky,

. . . The cruise this year has been in some respects much better than last and in others much worse. I haven't told the folks of the problems because Mom, as you know, really doesn't understand and worries a lot. We have lost two of our aircraft and one squadron mate to accidents. Actually two squadron buddies as one was injured such that he was sent home and one was killed. In addition, we've had more accidents than a squadron usually has in 2-3 cruises, and none of these were due to combat damage.

Yesterday was a stand-down day. You see, there are several carriers on the line at the same time. Each has different operating hours, therefore someone is usually operating at any given time of the day. In addition every 8-10 days one of the carriers does not launch any A/C. . . . I don't have many more flying days left of this line period. After visiting Japan we will have one more line period (30 days), then leave for home by way of Australia, New Zealand, and Brazil. . . .

Luckily Lynn and I have been able to take advantage of her job compensations and she has been able to meet me in several of our ports this year, St. Thomas, Rio, Manila, Hong Kong, and hopefully Tokyo. . . . We probably won't be home for Christmas, but the important thing to us is we will be together. There were times on this cruise when people were rumoring we wouldn't get home till after the first of the year. . . .

Actually the military does have some advantages, but if you ever go in, do it as an officer. I can't believe what the enlisted life is like sometimes. . . 'Am counting the days till this cruise is over. See you.

Love, Edward

On 5 September the last U. S. offensive began in Vietnam. True to his word, President Nixon was steadily winding down our presence in the country. By the end of the year our troop level would be down 280,000.

10 September 1970, Bad Reichenhall

Dear Mom & Dad,

    . . . I am so sorry to hear about Duane; it must be very hard for the Sparrows. . .

    The weather is good today, so we spent the morning riding around taking pictures. We rode out to Karlstein, a little village in the rear part of the folds of the mountains. We climbed up to the little church on the hill with is lit up at night. The ruins on the adjoining peak are apparently inaccessible at the present. We took a winding footpath through the mountains to Thum Lake. It is gorgeous country. I wish I had color film. Some of the trails we were on were pretty rough too, so we really had fun zooming down them on our bikes. We then went to Castle Grundstcin on the hill overlooking Reichenhall. It is a nice little castle, now used for apartments.

    October 1st we are moving to an apartment in a nice pension ("guesthouse", similar to a bed and breakfast) on the hill toward Bayrisch-Gmain. It is a really neat room with heat, hot running water, service, bath, decent toilet. It is infinitely better than the little hole we are in now.

    We have been tracting individual homes lately on the outskirts of town. You tend to meet some pretty rude people that way and we have been shouted at and run off the property a couple times now. Tracting is fun because you meet such a variety of characters. Then you meet the one or two neat people and they make up for all the trolls and orcs you run across.

    I've seen so many things over here that look like they're just right out of the "Trilogy", I can't believe it. For instance, we were coming home from Br. Nikisch, who lives several miles away when a thunderstorm came up, as is common here in summer evenings. It was the most beautiful lightning I've ever seen. All colors, red, blue, purple, silhouetting the jagged peaks in licking flames of beauty. And there are a lot of little cottages, which, if set into the side of a hill, could well pass for Hobbit holes. . .

Love, Rod

18 September 1970, Bad Reichenhall

The other day we spoke with Sr. Schäfer's mother. Apparently Sr. Schäffer raved about her experience at church, inviting her mother to come with them next time. The mother had previously not been interested. Schäfers will definitely be baptized eventually. We also resumed contact with Herr Ulrich, our bearded school teacher who was on vacation in Scandinavia. He is very intelligent and understands the concepts well.

We heard the Vienna Boys' Choir in Salzburg last week in the Mozarteum. Those boys can sure sing. Their lead soprano is especially good. The next day we had a work day in Salzburg and were very tired. A good part of the day before we had spent on our bikes, running around Karlstein and Reichenhall taking pictures. This is such an incredibly beautiful area we are working in. We also spent a couple pleasant evenings with Br. Schubert recently. The other night we watched films of his vacations in Greece and Italy and ate ice cream.

Sunday I spoke to the branch in Braunau at their Sacrament Meeting. . .

18 September 1970, Bad Reichenhall

Dear Mom & Dad,

. . . In the evening (of the work day) we had a short meeting at Br. Deng's, who lives in an apartment in the *Festung*, the fortress over the city. It was really neat. The *Festung* was never conquered. . . .

We have another sister here, Joan Rhodes. She is a student from California, studying for six weeks here at the Goethe Institute, a school for German. She is very nice, a junior in college, and restricted to a wheelchair due to a bone disease. She doesn't get to see as much as she ought because of the chair, so we are going to escort her around Reichenhall and show the sights. Sundays she goes to church with the Schuberts.

Well, by the time you get this it will almost be time for your trip to the temple. I can't say how happy I am about this. In the depressing moments, it's the memories of experience like those in the temple and thoughts of future reunions which provide the necessary strength. . . . Rod

21 September 1970, Portland

Darling,

Last night we got our recommends signed by Don Wood— 1st signature of his as the new President of the Portland Stake (in Pres. Emmett's place). Just one year ago last night you baptized me as your first baptism as a missionary—I guess I just like to make "Firsts" for everyone. Yes, at conference in the morn they announced Don Wood as Pres and Mel Randall as 1st Counselor. How about that? . . . Mom

Chapter 10

21 September 1970, at sea East of Taiwan

Dear Ricky,

. . . 'Sounds like you are enjoying this location much better than the last. I only hope you are able to take full advantage of the position you are in now and don't postpone "'til later", as so many of us do. But I guess very few people can be told what to do, instead we must find out for ourselves, which, if you consider it, is part of growing up. But on the other hand, it's not understanding what we have been taught over the years. After all if everyone had to learn from experience in every facet of our knowledge, knowledge would begin and end with each generation. . . .

We finished our fourth line period the 17th and left the area the 19th. We've been in Nationalist Chinese waters for the past couple of days doing some limited flying and entertaining guests. We will fly tomorrow and the next couple of days west of Okinawa, then on for a few days in the waters north of South Korea. After that we will put into the port of Yokosuka, which is not very far from Tokyo. I'm hoping that Lynn will be able to join me there, but since Duane's death I haven't received very much about her future plans.

'Just saw the flight schedule for tomorrow and my pilot and I are on it. You see we (ideally) pair up with one pilot during the training cycle (that's our shore time plus the short cruise) and stay together throughout the cruise. Ted Pratt and I fly together most of the time.

A few days ago, just before the end of the line period, a couple of the guys flew to Udorn Thailand where they called the Bureau to find out any information they could about the orders for the gents getting out of the squadron (rotating) after this cruise. . . Gene Williamson is going to be an admiral's aide. He will leave the squadron during the middle of the next line period. The rest of us will probably detach in December or January . . . (I will be going) to VX-4 which is a test and evaluation squadron at Pt. Mugu Calif about 75 miles north of Los Angeles on the coast. . . . That would require an extension of about 1 and a half years. I don't know, Little Brother. I'm really worrying about what to do. At a time like this one wants to be with people who would be affected by such a decision. When you fall in love and marry you may understand what's bothering me. (Also) the industry for which all my training and experience has been in is extremely depressed right now. Aero engineers are driving taxies, digging ditches, etc. And Duane's death really was a blow to Lynn as it was to all her family. Although she hasn't said too much about the subject I'm writing except that whatever I decide will be ok by her, I know she worries a great deal about it. I try to convince her that it's not dangerous, but am not even fooling myself.

I apologize for getting on a band wagon, Ricky. It's just that I really haven't expressed these feeling in this light as yet to anyone in the family and thought you the best one to open up to. Please don't mention anything that would disturb the folks.

Must go for now. Take care.

Edward

25 September 1970, Bad Reichenhall

Yesterday in Salzburg we had an interview conference with President Broberg. He is a great fellow and it was very good to see him. He told me that Br. Graham and I would remain in Reichenhall probably another two months. This is surprising because 20 elders are going home before Christmas and the total force is being reduced from 120 to 100 missionaries, so there will be transfers to re-adjust. He indicated he felt it was real inspiration that we were put there and expects that we will see a real breakthrough very soon. We know we will be seeing success. Today is his birthday, so we gave him a cake, baked by Sr. Zechmann. That evening we debated a Jehovah's Witness. This JW was pretty dumb, though, didn't even know his own doctrines, so it was not much fun. Two scriptures were enough to get him so confused that he said he was "insulted" and invited us to leave. Later we spent a pleasant evening with the Bocks, watching a documentary about Mussolini on TV. They are good people and ought to be members.

Today is my parents' 30th wedding anniversary, and today they were sealed in the Salt Lake Temple. I am so happy for them. I told Pres. B. about it and he was very happy as well. . . . I can see how God is directing this great work, his dealings with me, my family, and my friends—it is all a testimony to me.

We have been meeting with a good reception here and speaking to many good people. (I have been having trouble with my liver, which has caused considerable pain. I am scheduled to see a doctor about it.) . . . God's sheep will hear His voice and be gathered out.

25 September 1970, Bad Reichenhall

Dear Mom & Dad,

. . . Congratulations to Pres. Wood and to your firsts! Pres. Monson had told me about Pres. Emmett's new calling as Regional Representative. . . .

I can't say how happy I am about my family. I have been truly blessed and it is a real thrill to see the Gospel influencing our lives. I know it is true. . .

Love, Rod

28 September 1970, *Milano*

Dear Rod,

Ciao! . . . From your letter it is easy to see that you are all fired up and excited about the work in Austria. I'm positive that success will be yours as you continue to serve the Lord with diligence and in the spirit of giving. The Italian Church is really beginning to grow and prosper. The Lord is blessing the Italian Saints with great blessings because of their diligence and faithfulness in living His commandments. Their desire to share the glad tidings of the gospel with their friends, neighbors, and relatives is being paid by a great increase in baptisms with the work intensifying daily.

The program that is bearing the greatest yield is the member-mission program. We are almost entirely on a referral type program because of the help received from our members. The main thing that is involved in getting the members involved in the work is just that—getting them excited and involved with the program. In short: you must teach them to be missionaries by challenging them to produce and putting projects in their hands to show them that you have their trust. It takes a lot of time and concentration but the fruits are great.

Right now we are trying hard to present families the Family Home Evening program. This means giving them family oriented door approaches or making appointments with families for Family Home Evening in which you teach them what a FHE is and how to do it. We try to do this as soon after a first lesson as possible and many times even before we mention one thing about doctrine and beliefs. We are especially interested in fathers. We are trying hard to come up with ways to interest the family heads so that the family when baptized will be a unit complete with a leader who can hold the priesthood and take them to the temple. I have devised a book which had been very effective in both teaching FHEs and interesting the father so enclosed in this letter are the plans for the book. Maybe you will want to try it.

It is easy to use this kind of approach here in Italy for the people are very family oriented and love their children very much. The Catholic Church has done a tremendous job of preparing the people for the gospel. . . . The only trouble is that it has also prepared the people for communism and atheism. I have no fear, however, for God will prepare the hearts of the humble and meek. . . . The Lord is guiding the work here in Italy as he is throughout Europe and the world. I know that as we are faithful and diligent we will be blessed with many choice spirits to teach and baptize—He led my companion and me to two fine saints this month. I know this is the work of the Lord and it is the greatest work in the world! . . .

Much love, your brother, John Smurthwaite

30 September 1970, Portland

Dear Rod:

. . . I had a great thrill on the 25th of September to be able to go through the Temple with your mother and father. It was tremendous to see them sealed for time and all eternity. Now it will be possible for you to be sealed to them when you return from your mission. . . .

It is great to have 4 tremendous missionaries in the field now form the 15th Ward. You and Don and of course, Randy Rowley is in Japan and Jeff Wood is now in the East English Mission. We have two more to go before very long, Doug Visceri. . . will be going to the North English Mission and last night Brad Fackrell came to my home and informed me that he wanted to go on a mission and he will be taking his physical today. . . . By the first of the year Mitch Golden informs me that he wants to go on a mission and of course, Lee Middleton wants to go . . .

Clyde M. Waddell

Mom and Dad's trip to the Salt Lake City Temple affected many others, Dad's older brother, Raile Saxey and his wife, Mildred, were sealed as well, but the trip involved many friends and relatives. By way of explanation of the following letter, Reed, Mary, Joanne, and Maurine are Raile and Mildred's grown children. Faye is Dad's older sister. Throughout the family there are varying degrees of church activity. On the other side of the family, Helene is Mom's cousin and Aunt Carrie is her mother's sister. Mom was born in Boise, Idaho.

30 September 1970, Portland

Dearest One,

. . . The Temple trip was wonderful—a little heaven on earth for a few hours. We arrived there at 7 am and left at 12:40 pm—Geneal Wood, her Mother, Clyde, Eudora, Alfords, Raile and Mildred, besides us in our party. . . .

(The night before we had dinner with the Waddells) at *The Athenian*, a Greek place, very beautiful all in white and royal blue. . . . We watched the choir practice at Temple Square, then went with the Alfords to the Visitors Center. . . . I didn't sleep all nite, I was so keyed up. Mildred and Raile arrived at 6 am while we were getting ready.

We arrived at the Temple as the first party. After we had been there only a few minutes people started coming. It's sure a busy place. Everyone looked like angels in white. We really were very thrilled with it all. Only wish you'd been there to go with us.

After we had told them all goodbye Raile took the 4 of us out for brunch at *The Coachman*. After we got to their place in Provo, Reed and family brought us a fancy cake that was written "Congratulations Mom & Dad, Willie & Ed". Joanne and family came over and brought a bouquet of red and white flowers. Maurine took us for a tour of the BYU campus. There have been buildings completed to be dedicated this month.

Saturday morning we went for a ride, then Mary and her family came to call and we brought Faye out for the day. In the evening Dad and Raile and Joanne's husband went to the (BYU) football game (we lost).

Sunday morning early we left for home. Called Helene and family when we went thru Boise. Aunt Carrie was having a celebration for her 90th birthday. We stayed in Baker Sunday nite. . . .

I wanted you to know it was wonderful. We loved every minute of it. . . .

Love you Dearly, Mom

1 October 1970, Bad Reichenhall

Today we celebrated our Hump Day—one year of our mission completed. In the morning Br. Freckleton and Allen came over from Salzburg and we had a study class. Tonight we bought a nut cake and took it to the Schuberts where we had a fondue dinner. He makes it a little differently, with lots of different sauces to dip the meat in. It was a pleasant evening with plenty of humor.

It's been so cold the past week and a half; Monday morning we just couldn't take it anymore, so moved like little beavers to get from Schödtlweg (the cave) to Steilhofweg. They were kind to let us move in a little early. This is a wonderful Wohnung with hot running water and heating. It is a pleasant, modern apartment in a Pension on the hill towards Bayrisch Gmain overlooking Bad Reichenhall. The view is magnificent. It is warm and dry and modern and pleasant. It is so much better than our old place, which was really awful—cold, damp, and dark. We ride a wonderful street down the hill at 60mph past the Goethe Institute.

This past year has been quite an experience. I cannot say I have been always happy. In fact, at times it's been miserable, but pride and stubbornness kept me from quitting. I have grown a lot though, and I know that this is truly the work of the Lord. If it were not, we missionaries would have ruined it long ago.

4 October 1970, Bad Reichenhall

Friday we went to Salzburg. In the evening we saw "Geschichten aus dem Wiener Wald", a very good play, though a bit risqué in places. It is a biting social critique of Austria, Germany, and the Catholic Church. It was very well done, but the audience seemed unresponsive, perhaps because it struck so close to home. . . .

We took the midnight train to Innsbruck, caught two hours of sleep on the train, then stood in the Innsbruck Bahnhof for a couple hours watching the jugos (Yugoslavians) and bums making passes at the girls. We took a walk around Innsbruck to find an eating joint, but nothing was open. So we starved.

Saturday we had a good missionary conference and in the afternoon had a work day. I was with Sr. Bateman and Br. Jones. In the evening the branches had a talent night. Sunday was District Conference, after which we took the train home. It was exhausting, with very little food.

So long as it did not detract from our missionary work we were encouraged to attend cultural events, including plays and concerts, as part of our general education, both to know the culture better and to become personally more refined; *Geschichten* may have been stretching it a bit. Mission rules have become generally more strict over the years and vary somewhat from mission to mission depending on local conditions and experience.

7 October 1970, *Milano*

Dear Rod,

. . . Missionary work in Italy is really booming, as it is elsewhere in Europe. The missionaries and members are really being blessed here in this most fruitful field of labor. . .

The Lord has been good to me as well, blessing me with the opportunity of baptizing three very fine saints and assisting in others. My labor is continually a source of great joy and happiness to me. I continually rejoice to think that the Lord has called me to serve Him here in Italy. We have been blessed so greatly, haven't we! . . .

Next month our mission offices are moving to Rome. It could mean the mission might be divided (rumor). There are also about 31 new greenies coming in before the 15th of September. I've had a greenie for about the last 5 months here in *Milano*, and I think I might be going on to some other city soon. . . .

John

p.s. 'Met a whole lot of Portlanders the other day. All Mormons! One is the Stake President's wife from your stake. They were really cool and great fun to talk to.

9 October 1970, Bad Reichenhall

Dear Mom & Dad,

. . . (Preparing to fill out readmission application for BYU,) I have a problem as far as a major is concerned. Archaeology is definitely out. English, History, Philology, Anthropology? I just don't know. What is the market like back home for teachers? Which levels, which subjects are in demand, or will be in demand?

(The doctor checked my labs.) He said I have a case of posthepatitic hyperbilirubinemia, nothing to get worried about. . . . Mom, could you send me some Vitamin C? Going into winter now, I would like to have some help.

The leaves are turning here and it is gorgeous. The mountains are covered with deciduous trees. It snowed on the mountain tops and the air is brisk. Our new apartment is great though, except it is so nice we have a tendency to oversleep. It is the first decent apartment I have had in Europe. . .

We gave Br. Ulrich, our investigator, a Fifth Discussion (Plan of Salvation) the other night. It was really great and at the end he said the prayer. He is doing just fine and should be baptized, hopefully before we are transferred.

Say, what do you do against thinning hair? I am going bald—receding hairline, the whole bit. . . .

Love, Rod

16 October 1970, Bad Reichenhall

The past little while has been uneventful. We have been working on a lot of miscellaneous projects, with less tracting. Two new investigators have been added to the list: Frau Blanck and Familie Riedl. . . .

This has been a pleasant time for us, marked by considerable thinking about home and the future. It does not feel the same as being "trunkey", and we do not feel too guilty about it—it is more a matter of taking stock and reflecting.

Today we took Joan to the top of the Predigtstuhl, the big mountain to the west of Reichenhall with a cable car up to the top.

The view was magnificent. It was cold, though, and we could not do much with the wheelchair, so we came down again after a short time.

My relationship with Edward has become stronger and he has seen fit to confide that his worst problem just now is whether to accept orders for another assignment or not. I regret very much that I have not known my older brothers better, for I now feel a strong love for them both.

16 October 1970, Bad Reichenhall

Dear Mom & Dad,

. . . We tracted out the Riedl family. A grandma came to the door and said she was busy taking care of the kids and the parents weren't home. As we went around the house to leave, however, we looked in the kitchen in time to see the mother pop down behind the counter. Not very well hidden, hand showing. We gave a tract to a little kid there with strict orders to run in and give it to Mommy. She did. Then, as we continued tracting, people started referring this family to us. ("Do you know someone interested in religion?" "Sure, Family Riedl.") We expected trouble, but went back in the evening. "Probably JWs," we thought. After much stalling, postponing, and hemming and hawing, they let us in. We were shocked—they were friendly. In fact, they are golden, despite the fact he is on the Lutheran Layman's Council.

We've also found a very nice lady, Frau Blanck. She took a *Book of Mormon* well and promised to read. She is one of the most enthusiastic investigators we've seen. I told you, we finally got Ulrick to pray? We've had good luck lately getting people to pray in our discussions.

My glasses finally gave up the ghost and broke in two. I went to Salzburg and got new frames for eight dollars. They look really good and are stronger than the old ones. How does that price compare with America? . . .

Love, Rod

19 October 1970, Portland

Dearest Rod:

. . . Brad Fackrell's mission call came through and he's going to Japan in a week or so. . . . You knew Tracey Hill was in a Norwegian Mission didn't you? . . . Don has his first family to baptize on Oct 31st. Hope your new golden family works out well. . . .

Mom

23 October 1970, Bad Reichenhall

I feel sad tonight because my time in Austria is half-over and I feel that I have accomplished very little. A mission is really eine Entwicklungssache, *a matter of development. The Lord could get this work done other ways, but for our sake, He gives us the chance to develop ourselves in His service. Comparing the present me with the former me with the could-have-been me, I feel defeated at my lack of progress. Where is the success, and where is the joy? I feel like a failure.*

Another brief epoch in my life is almost over, as I expect not to be much longer here. It is indeed unusual that Br. G and I have lasted together so long. I have much the same feeling now as I had the last couple weeks in Wels. It is rather a feeling of de-nouement, of wrapping up. Summer has ended and winter snows have begun; certain events and persons in our work, like Br. Hartmann, have reached their conclusion; Joan goes home tomorrow. Those things that have characterized my time in Bad Reichenhall are vanishing before my eyes. How I will miss these people and these places I have come to love so dearly!

23 October 1970, Bad Reichenhall

Dear Mom & Dad,

. . . All of our appointments with investigators fell through. Wednesday we had a study class and half day workday in Braunau. I got to work with Br. R, a really sharp fellow who came out with our group, the Big 18. That was fine except he lost his passport so we spent the whole day looking for it. When our group came last December 4th it was the biggest shipment of missionaries Austria has ever received. Dividing us into the mission took a huge transfer codenamed "Big Ben" in which almost every pair in the country was changed. There are only 16 of the 18 still here. One brother went home at about 4 months out. . . He worried himself right out of his mind. The other Br. went out after about 10 months. He was a very good friend of mine and a mutual friend of Bilbo. He evidently had been too much "worried about" at home, and here he let little imagined errors get to him. I felt sorry to see him go, but he had persuaded himself he couldn't take it, and I guess Pres. Monson agreed. The 16 left, distributed more or less evenly through the mission, are among the best here though. Br. Duke, my good friend from the LTM and Wels, is in the mission home recovering from bronchitis.

There has been snow on the mountains, now almost down to our level. Western Austria, most of south Germany, Switzerland, and northern Italy, all have snow; mountain passes are being closed. And it is only October.

I have prepared a flip book for introduction of the Family Home Evening program and tried it out at the Schubert's last night. He was in Salzburg on church business, so we kept company with Sis. Schubert until he returned, watching an old movie. It was pretty neat; and boy were they enthused about the flip book. Saturday we will present the FHE to *Familie* Riedl.

I'm afraid I gave Br. Allen a lot of food for thought the other day as we rode home from Braunau. He is a great fellow, but has a tendency to give the benefit of the doubt too much, occasionally missing the fact that there are lots of things in this old world which are abominable from the start. . . . Generally speaking, this people is a varied mixture of nature-worshippers, atheists, and idol-worshippers. . . (T)here is very little difference between a mass held by a Catholic priest and the mumbo-jumbo of an African medicine man. There is very little difference between the nature-worship of a New Zealand aboriginal and a German except one wears more clothes. And atheism is atheism in any case. Mind you, the people aren't evil, but they have been deceived by some evil philosophies . . . (The) people are inherently good. . . .

Love, Rod

30 October 1970, Bad Reichenhall

Dear Mom & Dad,

Wednesday we spent in Salzburg Christmas shopping. Due to a case of bad connections we ended up spending the whole day there instead of just half a day. . . .

The leaves are gorgeous here just now. This is the most colorful Autumn I have ever seen. Today we dashed around and snapped a few pictures of hillsides and things. It is terrific.

Last Sunday there weren't many in church because half the branch went to the temple in Switzerland. It was the first time for a lot of them, including good *Familie* Jäger. They were really impressed and happy. I gave a talk in Sacrament Meeting. It was about the best one I have done—everyone complemented me afterwards, and that is unusual in Austria. They don't generally complement missionaries on talks. One little old lady bugged me for ten minutes afterwards, talking about my "sermon".

We finally got our copies of the new, revised dialogues (discussions). They have really improved a lot. Many of the difficult parts have been changed. The German is a lot better, too. Now we have to memorize them.

One of the good brethren in Salzburg, Gerald Roth, has been called to the North Britain Mission. The funny thing about his call is there was no date given. It said simply, "write the mission president so he will know when you are coming". . .

Br. Graham and I are sitting on pins and needles this week. There should be a big transfer. (Can you believe it—Br. Archibald is going home.) One of us will probably be moved, but this area is too good to leave, dash it all! . . .

Love, Rod

Chapter 11

29 October 1970, on Yankee Station

Dear Folks,

Thanks much for your letters. Mail calls seem few and far between anyway without missing one, as I'm sure you are well aware, Dad. . .

The weather has really been terrible here this line period. We've had two typhoons chase us out of the Gulf, are in the middle of a tropical storm now, and another typhoon is only a couple days away. It's ok by me because it means very little flying—but that's not so good either as it makes the time really drag. Am really looking forward to getting home to my wife. . . .

Love, Edward

5 November 1970, Portland

Dear Rod:

Greetings from Portland and the greatest Stake in the Church!

. . . We are reorganizing our Stake Missionary Program and plan having the greatest Stake Mission in the Church. Next year at this time we will be leading the church in convert baptisms. I had a wonderful experience this summer teaching a special class of men and women who were preparing to go to the Temple. I am sure your parents discussed some of the experiences we had together. They were in this group and largely contributed to the sweet spirit which prevailed there. I was so happy that they had the opportunity to go through the Salt Lake Temple. . . .

Talking about missionaries, you know Randy is in Japan. Brad Fackrell just received a call to Japan. Jeffrey is in England on the coast near Dover . . . You know, of course, that Stephen Hill is in Germany and Tracey is in Norway. There are about six other Elders from our Stake I have just set apart within the last month and several more coming up so our Stake is being well represented. Everyone here at home is fine. . . . President Wood

6 November 1970, Braunau am Inn

Well, transfers came and I was called as the new Branch President of Braunau am Inn. Br. Freckleton called us about noon on the 2nd , saying they would be closing Bad Reichenhall. We dashed down to the Grossgmain Post and called Pres. Broberg to confirm it. Sure enough, the response in Reichenhall had been such that, what with the cut-back in missionaries in Austria, it had to be closed. We were really sad about that, for we had come to love the town and our wonderful people there. Br. Graham was sent to Innsbruck. Tuesday night we received the transfer and found it was for the 4th rather than the 5th, so we had to really hurry. That night we ate with the Bock's. At the end he bore his testimony and admonished us to stay strong. Then they gave us a couple of fossils from Untersberg, the resting place of Kaiser Karl behind Walser Feld. Last Sunday we had our last dinner with the Schuberts. We had dropped by to take pictures of them just as they returned from the Konditorei with pieces of cake. They invited us in to help eat the cake and then invited us for dinner later: a sort of shishkebab with fried potatoes and lots of ketchup.

I was not at all happy about leaving Reichenhall, and am not terribly enthusiastic at being President in Braunau. Parts of Austria can be quite primitive compared to what we had become accustomed to, and Braunau looks like one of those towns where missionaries can go to seed. But being aware of that from the beginning may help to avoid it.

Braunau am Inn is a pleasant old town similar to Wels, built as a fortified trading center along the river Inn, the northern border; it was especially important in the ancient salt trade coming north from Salzburg. Its companion German town is Simbach, just over the bridge. Large flocks of swans live along the river as well and flock to the park between the old city walls and the riverbank. They are black when first hatched, incidentally, and turn white over time. The branch met in a little retail building with storefront, rooms for classes, and a small apartment in the second floor where the missionaries lived.

6 November 1970, Braunau

Dear Mom & Dad,

. . . The last branch president, Br. Lundberg, had been sick with the flu and sure enough, within a day or two I had it too. Last night I was up all night with a bad fever which broke during the night. I'm not too bad today, with just cold sweats. As long as I'm lying down it's okay. By tomorrow I will be fine. The mission is having us all get flu shots so as to cut down on the illness this winter. Last winter everyone was sick. We were supposed to get them last week, but it did not work out, so we will have to wait until next week. . . .

My new companion is Br. R, from North Dakota, another of the Big 18. I have had good luck staying with our brethren from the LTM; they are a great group.

I have doubts about this assignment, though. It's unbelievable how much work there is to do here, how many things there are to take care of. And then there are the church courts coming up, which I will have to handle. I don't relish having to sit with the brethren in judgment. . .

Love, Rod

We don't call them "church courts" anymore; they are Disciplinary Councils. The modern name more accurately reflects what they are about. The objectives are to help people repent by relieving them of guilt and duty, support any injured parties, and protect the functioning and reputation of the Church. There are three possible outcomes: dismissal (the member stays in full fellowship, perhaps with counseling or other guidance if needed), disfellowship (which means limiting participation for a time), and excommunication (which means removal of membership and loss of blessings, but also relief from responsibilities of membership). All our cases were for apostasy, not just being inactive, of course, but actually leaving the Church and speaking against it or joining some other religion. These had been stalled in Braunau for a simple reason—missionaries led the Branch there, and missionaries expect to bring people into the Church, not take them out.

6 November 1970, Klagenfurt, Austria

Dear Sax,

I don't have any idea where you are so I'll just have to write and hope it gets there. I thought I'd write and tell ya that I'm now in Klagenfurt (the coldest city in Austria). Can you believe that we have been in Austria almost a year? This thanksgiving and xmas look just as promising as last year as far as "Darhubers" and "Rotheneders" are concerned (they had fed us well and were great cooks). The members are really great.

I've decided I'm going back to the "Y" next fall—maybe we'll see each other before then. I'll let you know how xmas goes. Keep up the good work pal, and let me know if you get this card, ok?

Br. Fager

9 November 1970, Ranshofen

Liebe Brüder!

Danke für den geistlichen Besuch. Trotz Bier war ein guter Gedanke da. Ich spürte es an den Äusserungen meines Mannes.

Liebe Grüsse,

Eure Sr. E. Dzugan

(Dear Brethren!

Thanks for the ministerial visit. Despite beer there were good thoughts there. I felt it in the expressions of my husband.

Loving Greetings,

Your Sister E. Dzugan)

Sister Erna Dzugan was not actually a member, but was a friend to the missionaries. She would long ago have joined but for the objections of her husband, who drank heavily and was controlling. She was a good-hearted, sweet lady with two fine teenagers and a strong need to talk, especially about philosophy, the nature of the soul, our relationship to God, and the virtue of Platonic love, *Nächstenliebe*, love of neighbor. They lived in the country on a tree farm a short bus-ride or long bike-ride from Braunau.

The Klingers were another couple of "professional investigators" who were very kind to the missionaries. They lived in Braunau in a sweater factory and were among the most entrepreneurial people we met, something they proudly attributed to the fact that they were actually German, not Austrian. National and ethnic differences could be difficult to decipher, however, for the border had shifted several times through the centuries.

9 November 1970, Braunau

Braunau is nicknamed "Sweater City" by the missionaries because they always come here to buy sweaters from the Klinger's, who make them at very reasonable rates. My first few tests here are over. We have visited all the active members and introduced me, though we are all a little acquainted from former visits. They don't seem to like me very much, especially my new companion, Br. R. He is quite trunked-out and seems not to want to work. His German is not awful, and I suppose his discussions are okay, though I have not heard them. He and Lundberg got along famously together, so he is not enthusiastic about having a new companion, especially one who really wants to work as I do. No doubt we will work things out as time passes.

Sunday we had a very embarrassing experience. The brethren Jackson and Willmann (the Zone Leader from Innsbruck) were here visiting us, so in the afternoon we used their car to visit members in further areas with the ZL's car. We also gave a little Sunday School lesson to Sr. Jetzlsperger in St. Georgen. Br. R said the Sacrament Meeting was at 7:30, so when we came back to town we bought a torte, then went over to Klinger's. At 7:15 we returned to the church to find the members had started without us! Br. Baumgartner was giving a talk and Br. K, who has a serious Word of Wisdom problem, was conducting the meeting. I did not know what to think—had they formed their own church? I walked up to the stand and sat down in my place as Br. K called the meeting to close. Before we started singing I asked him what had happened and he informed me the Sacrament Meeting is always at 5:45. R had blown it! Badly! I let them proceed with the close. This is the way we make good impressions on the members in the mission field.

10 November 1970, Portland

My Darling Br. Pres,

Congratulations—I am so proud of you and we are anxiously awaiting your letter. . . You are in a beautiful country, so much color and charm. Enjoy it! Isn't Braunau where Hitler was born? . . . Mom

Indeed it is.

Prior to marrying Mom in 1940, Dad roomed in Portland with an Austrian family named Poltz. He raved about the wonderful dinners Mrs. Poltz made, especially the soups and dumplings—*knödel*, which I also came to love. They listened to the news on the radio during or after dinner and often heard reports about Hitler, with excerpts from his speeches. Mr. Poltz would snort, shake his head, and mutter, "My countryman!"

It no doubt was easier for Austrian expats to recognize the Nazis for what they were than it was for those still in Austria. A myth was propagated after the war that the *Anschluss,* the unification, was forced upon an unwilling country and that most engaged in silent resistance to the German administration. In fact, resistance was very silent indeed, and the myth served mainly to salve the consciences and wounded pride of those at the time and their immediate families, and to please the occupation forces.

Many Austrians, especially those in government and positions of power and influence, welcomed union with their more powerful cousins to the north, and saw the *Anschluss* as an opportunity for greater power, influence, and wealth. This was demonstrated by the rapidity with which the government adopted the trappings of their new masters: annexation was announced over the radio in the evening, was official at midnight, and the next morning the swastika was hanging from every flagpole and was worn on every policeman's arm. Everything was prepared well in advance, even while the government proclaimed its opposition.

As missionaries we met with all political persuasions, including a rare unreconstructed and unrepentant Nazi whose only regret was that they did not win. Most who had been through the war remembered it with deep sorrow for the suffering, loss, and waste it entailed; many had been to the Russian front and a number of them had been prisoners. For them, the memories were bitter and they suppressed them when they could, an inefficient balm.

Only now, almost seventy years later, are the few remaining Austrians and Germans from that time period and their descendents coming to terms with the events of that tragic history. In 1970 the myth remained in full force. It is said that there are no atheists in foxholes, but the fact is that two men in a foxhole, experiencing exactly the same trials, can emerge in opposite directions: one becomes an embittered, misanthropic atheist; the other becomes a priest who dedicates his life to service and love of God. For one, human suffering proves there is no God, for the other, the testimony of the Spirit in the midst of suffering proves there is one. The difference is what is in the heart, and what the heart chooses.

13 November 1970, Innsbruck

Hey *Du*!

I just lost my first Junior. He's in *Wien*. Bro Bill Summers is now here; co-seniors again. I've already ridden that bike more here than the entire time in Reichenhall, and cold! Wow! It's cold except today it's warmed up. Today we're throwing a surprise birthday party for both sisters. Today's Robinson and next week is Bateman's. Summers and I are going looking for a gym this morning. He brought a basketball. Innsbruck is cool and I've already spoken in Sac. Meeting which lasts 45 min. to an hour. We have a double burner that we use for breakfast. This place is rough. Monday we hit doors for 8 hrs. and spoke to one person. Don't loaf too much!

Graham

14 November 1970, Salzburg

Events move fast these days. At the moment I am at dinner in the Peter's Keller *in Salzburg after a morning of most revealing and beneficial interview conferences with Pres. Broberg. He indicated some wonderful things and expressed great confidence in me, which of course made me feel good. He said my special assignment in Braunau is to find a member there who can be entrusted with most of the branch work. He explained that missionaries have spent far too much time with the members in Braunau and we are not to do that. Braunau is a difficult town and has not been productive. He did not indicate that I would baptize there, but said I could and that I was chosen for the job because of my experience and capability, as well as to give me more experience. As for Br. R and me, well, we still do not get along well.*

14 November 1970, Braunau

Dear Mom and Dad,

. . . I like Pres. Broberg more each time he comes around. Sis. Broberg was with him this time too and she talked to each of us individually about health, food, apartments, etc.

. . . . It looks like living will be a lot cheaper here than in Reichenhall. Rent is $10 compared with $24 there; meals are substantially less, though travel to Salzburg every week or two is considerably more. Anyway, I should be able to get by on $110 here with no problem, like I did in Wels.

Last Sunday the ZL from Innsbruck was here to work with us. After Sunday School (I teach the adult class and Br. R teaches the children's class) we visited members who live out of town. One is a little old sister, Sister Jetzlsperger, who lives at considerable distance on a farm. We give her a special little Sunday School class each week. . .

Most of the week I was still pretty sick with a cough and sore throat, but am well now. . . .

Love, Rod

14 November 1970, *Wien*

Hi Sam!

. . . How is it out in Braunau as *Gemeindevorsteher*? From what I hear, that's a great place there. A couple weeks ago I ordered some sweaters from one of your members there who was here in *Wien* delivering 16 beautiful sweaters to Br. Archibald (2 days before he flew home!) I'll bet he had fun at customs.

Things are going pretty good here. When I was still working in the 9th *Bezirk* we found a beautiful young family (28 years old with 2 young kids). The *Frau* got a testimony immediately and has read the B of M at least 2 times through. The only problem is her *Mann*. . . oh well, faith and patience. I know things will work out in this case. My first connection with a conversion on my mission. It's great!

So mentally and spiritually things are improving! Physically is something else. I feel a bit stronger now, and the cough is somewhat better, but it just won't give up. I will probably go back out in the field this week, but I would say the odds are about 75% that within 2 months I'll be in the States somewhere where my lungs like it better. I believe the whole thing is caused by a slight allergy to wool. No way to tell for sure, though, without tests, which I haven't done yet. Once in a while the ring gets heavy,

Sam—

I finally decided to quit worrying about it and accept whatever the Lord wants to do with me. I certainly have learned a lot here in the Mission Home. . . .

Believe it or not though, my PMA has actually improved during my stay here—maybe it's sleeping in till 8 o'clock and not needing to feel guilty about it!

Right now I'm sitting in the *Versand* taping "Finlandia" on my cassette. I'm going to have the most complete *Vortrag* and Music library when I leave this place.

Say, I don't think I ever apologized properly for all of the trouble I gave you in Wels when I was caught up in that "*Freude*" garbage. I'm sorry and I'm glad that I can call you a friend. I have long since repented of that program and I'm much happier for it. Thought you might like to know. . . .

See you soon,

Love, Frodo

17 November 1970, Portland

Dear Rod,

USS America started home 13 November. . . .

Mom

18 November 1970, Braunau

Br. R and I had quite a quarrel after pedaling back from Sr. Jetzlsperger's last Thursday. He certainly does not like me. Naja, *that's too bad; as long as we can get along well enough to get the work done. Last Friday, the 13th, we helped Klinger's, our perma- nent professional investigators, work on building a roof onto an old house in the* Altstadt *they had bought for their daughter and her husband. It was a good day full of hard work, more than I have done for a long time. Tonight our sisters had a Relief Society meet- ing, a very good one, with a lesson about Satan by Sr. Muehlbacher. Srs. Gebauer and Baumgartner spoke a lot, but Sr. Reiter came late and seemed embarrassed. The others gave her a bad time, which is unfortunate. She is a good woman; it seems Austrian nature (or is it simply human?) to heckle and kid, but I think many feelings are hurt that way.*

20 November 1970, Braunau

Dear Mom & Dad,

Last Sunday went pretty well, certainly better than the first Sunday. Br. and Sis. Weissenberger from Salzburg visited us in the afternoon. He was here for the quarterly review of the books. I can't believe how much there is to do here. We have a total of about 39 members, of which about 16-19 are at least somewhat active. The missionaries here before (and my comp's thinking has been too strongly influenced by the old bad habits) spent too much time visiting members so now as I try to ease out of it—under in- structions from Pres. Broberg—it is difficult. . . .

At any rate, to add to the natural difficulties of the job, Br. R has turned out to be a "trunk-out", one who thinks about home too much, etc., sits on the luggage which is already packed, and quite lazy. . . . Well, that's how it looks out here. . . .

Wednesday we had Study Class and District Meeting in

Salzburg again. There are only four in the District, Br. Freckleton, Allen, R, and I. We then had a workday there, which was really great. Br. Allen and I tracted out a house in the old part of the city there and got a "come back" for the afternoon. Freckleton and I went back, but the contact wasn't there, so we waited. It was a workshop for making candlesticks and art pieces according to old style and technique, and for restoring old art pieces. They were putting gold leaf on candlesticks while we were there. We asked about the house, which was clearly very old, and were informed it was built in the 1400s, but the little square workshop where they were working dated from Roman time. It had been used as a guard house in a series of fortifications. . . .

There aren't any investigators here, haven't been for a long time. How is that for luck: first in Wels, no baptisms for two years; then in Reichenhall, no baptisms since one year, and he has apostatized; and now Braunau. *Naja*, I guess I shouldn't complain. . . .

Love, Rod

23 November 1970, *Wien*

Dear Sam!

. . . My health is quite improved and I'm waiting for a spot to open up so I can go back out in the field. It seems I'm odd man in the mission right now. . . . I read where Pres. Wood was made Stake President up in Portland. I'll bet you're pleased about that. I know how much you respect Pres. Wood. . .

May the hair on your toes grow ever longer. (Say—Sis. Barlow was up here for the Sister's Conference, and I saw that she had a copy of *The Hobbit* with her! It's a small world.) . . . Frodo p.s. Have you ever heard from Herr Wist again?

No, I never did.

27 November 1970, Braunau

Dear Mom & Dad,

. . . Yes, we'll have a Christmas tree here in the church. Our church location is on the ground floor and our apartment is on the second floor, so it's almost like having one big apartment. The Relief Society is buying a tree. . . .

Last Wednesday we went around and visited our out-of-town members, as the weather was nice for a change. With our bikes to St. Georgen, then to Mattighofen, then back to Braunau. We left about 1:00 and got back about 7:00. Cold! Very! This is the second largest area which is handled by elders on bikes, the largest being Voralberg in the far west near Switzerland. . . .

Braunau is about the same sort of town as Wels, but only about half the size, about 17,000. There are a lot of neighboring towns and villages, though, so the practical population is somewhat more. . . . Rod

28 November 1970, Braunau

For Thanksgiving we rented a bus and went to Salzburg. There were eight of us: Sr. Reiter, Sr. Baumgartner, Sr. Gebauer and her sister, Sr. Dunner and Edeltraud, and the two of us. The missionaries in Salzburg had prepared a very good dinner with turkey, sweet potatoes, corn, and pumpkin pie. They also had a

program afterwards. Not all the Austrians liked the food; corn, af-
ter all, is for feeding the swine. Our biggest problem was with
fog—It slowed us down and made going dangerous.

It was sure good to see the Schuberts and Br Nestlinger,
and everybody from Salzburg. I had really grown to love that
branch. Schubert and I had a good talk about starting the Teacher
Trainer Course, Dad. I'm going to teach it here in Braunau start-
ing in January. . . .

Br. R and I have had a couple more quarrels. I have never
had so much trouble with anyone. Finally I called the President,
who told me just to be strong with him and follow the handbook.
That is the best counsel, anyway, though sometimes hard to follow.

29 November 1970, at Sea

Dear Folks,

I'm starting this letter now, but will not put it in an envelope until we arrive in Rio as we have no mail service until then
and I may want to add something. We pulled out of Sydney the
morning of 24 November and have been steaming almost due East
since. . . . The people (in Sydney) were extraordinarily kind to all.
It was a very friendly atmosphere, not too unlike that of the U.S. a
few years ago before Vietnam, etc. . . .

The carrier *The SangriLa* is about 600 miles south and a little east of our position since they are following a "great circle"
route between Sydney and South America. That way would be
shorter, but also much colder. We right now are encountering
moderate to heavy seas and cold winds, but if it's any consolation
to us the last message that was reported to us from *The SangriLa*
was that she was in heavy 13 foot seas with 2 inches of snow and

ice on the flight deck and icebergs in sight. So, I'm glad we are going the way we are, even if it is a little longer. . . .

We have been at sea 7 days because we had 2 November 26ths (both holidays on the ship) and have 11 days left before our next port. We haven't seen land since leaving the New Zealand area on our second day out and won't for 2-3 days when we round the tip of South America. You can take it from me, this is no fun! I'm sure you must remember your trips across the Atlantic, Dad, and know what I mean. But at least I've got a stateroom with only 5 other guys in with me. Though with all the goodies (presents and souvenirs, we've pretty much used up all the extra room. . . .

Love, Edward

4 December 1970, Braunau

Dear Mom & Dad,

One year ago today I arrived in Wels: my, how time flies! It is hard to believe. . . .

Yesterday we celebrated "*Krampus*" day, the day the evil demons come out with sticks and beat all the bad little children. Then Nicholas comes and gives candy and cookies to the good ones. We had a little supper and played games and all the children got bags of cookies, etc. Afterwards, some of the parents, the Baumgartners and Reiters, and we went "*kegeln*", the European version of bowling. That was all a lot of fun.

We went to a lot of work to decorate the three windows we have on our little church here. We put scenes of "snow" on them, one of Bethlehem, one of bells and "Merry Christmas", and one of a country church scene. Austrians don't generally do such things, so everyone who saw it "oohed and aahed" and became very excited about it. It did come out pretty good and we are quite happy about it. Frau Friedl, who owns a shop across the street, even asked us to do her window too. . . .

Just now we're preparing a Christmas program for Sunday School, trying to move on the church courts, and trying to get the missionary work on a decent footing here. . .

I see the Y offers a major in Comparative Literature. . . .I suppose that's "trunky" to think about it. *Naja*. ("*Naja*" in German is about like shrugging the shoulders and saying "oh well" in English. I say it a lot.) . . .

Love, Rod

5 December 1970, Itzehoe, Germany

Dear Rod,

Well, it sounds like things are going fine down in your neck of the woods. A little over a week ago I was sent here to Itzehoe with a "new elder" or "goldie" (no more "greenie") to re-open the city. Evidently it had quite a bad name before when the missionaries were here last ("It's-a-hole"). As you can see it was an original nickname, but we are going to change that. In our first week we have had 8 cottage meetings (meetings in members' homes where investigators can get acquainted with other church members as well as hear a gospel message), so I am not complaining at all. The city has great potential.

It was real hard leaving Hamburg after 6 months and *besonders* the family that was baptized, but the work goes on and I'm not indispensable. It did make me think, however, how hard it will be to leave next year. We'll have to come back and tour our missions together someday. The saints here are so great! As you mentioned in your letter, time goes by too quick and to think, it's been over a year since we've seen one another and we don't even have a year left here.

Rod, I want you to know how much I appreciate your friendship and how much I love you and what you are. *Gott sei mit dir*!

Love, Don

p.s. A couple of weeks ago Apostle Mark E. Peterson visited our stake conference and gave the whole stake a special challenge. . . . (He challenged the stake to hold Family Home Evenings, then invite non-members to FHE, then the missionaries to offer to help them hold their own FHE).

11 December 1970, Portland

Dear Rod:

Had a fine open house, good attendance and the priests did a fine job. Tomorrow I am baptizing Rose Spitzer's cousins, Mike and Cheryl. They are fine kids and understood all the lessons beautifully!

. . . Just heard Randy Rowley had 3 baptisms and Doug Visceri has been asked to spend Christmas with a family (in his mission)! . . .

With brotherly love, Russ Kenaga, Jr., Portland 15th Ward

18 December 1970, Braunau

Dear Mom & Dad,

Another week is past, Christmas is almost here, and we still don't have any snow. Last week it did snow a little, but quickly melted. Wednesday we went to Salzburg and they have a couple inches there already. Braunau just seems to be in the wrong place for snow. . . .

I think I mentioned I teach the adult Sunday School class. We have, theoretically, a Sunday School Superintendant, but he is in a state of semi-apostasy, so I act as Superintendant too. This is our biggest problem in the branch—no one wants to do anything, so the missionaries end up doing it all. In January I want to start a Teacher Trainer Course with the help of Br. Schubert. I hope it will enthuse people about working in the church as well as giving them basic principles of teaching.

. . . (Also, the) members of the branch will be divided into Home Teaching districts and as of January we will have an official Home Teaching Program again, something they haven't had for years. . . .

My biggest problem remains with my companion, though. I have never met anyone so critical or moody. From one hour to the next he can change from being rather friendly to a sullen steampot, ready to explode. And he generally does explode. I've spoken with Pres. Broberg and done my best to get along with the fellow, but it just doesn't seem to work. I have finally decided to write Pres. Broberg asking for a change of companion for the sake of our mental health and for the work here, which has certainly been affected by it. It is really a tick-off, after three great companions, to get a problem like this.

... We taught a family about the *Book of Mormon* the other night. It is a great family, the best looking investigators they have had in Braunau for a long time, and we're quite hopeful. ... Rod

21 December 1970, Portland

Dearest Rod,

Sunday we woke up to about 4 or 5 inches of snow. It looked like a winter wonderland. I stayed in bed all day. I had caught your Dad's bad cough. He's feeling pretty good again now and he put on his program for Sunday School. ...

Edward called from Austin, Texas, Friday night. Boy, I'm so happy he's back in the states—thank God! He's safe. He has joined for another 2 years though with the promise of staying stateside to test the new jet—F14 or some such. ...

Love, Mom

25 December 1970, Braunau

We have been pretty busy getting things ready for Christmas, but still managed to have time for a few more fights. He is very touchy.

On the 22nd we took a package of food and a present to Sr. Jetzlsperger in St. Georgen. We missed one train by a few seconds, but caught the next one, though it meant wolfing down our bean soup and "apple pie a-la-mode", which we bought at the Mühlbauer's. We had a pleasant celebration with Sr. J—sang songs and so forth. She gave us lots of cookies, cakes, and so forth.

The next day we had our branch Christmas party. . . We

presented the program sent to us by the church, with an enlarged portion for the children, for whom we built scenery, etc. They were quite taken with popcorn balls I made, which they had never had before, and with the popcorn chains on the tree. Overall turnout was poor because most couldn't come, but the "key people" were there and it was a booming success! I made popcorn balls and they loved them, having never seen them before. We made popcorn chains for the tree and also scenery for the children's part of the program. . . . That, along with the successful job we did on the window decorations made many say it had never been so beautiful before. Br. Reiter took me aside and said, "You've really shown us something tonight". I am confident of real success in the branch spirit and accomplishment in the coming 2-3 months, with this Christmas party as a push-off point.

The 24th we visited the Klinger's where we snacked and chatted, then to the Reiter's, where we decorated the tree and spent the evening. They apparently liked the job we did on the one at church. Over here the big event on Christmas is to be surprised with a decorated tree rather than to do the decorating, something children never do. So they were happy to have us decorate. The chief parts of the decorations are pieces of brightly wrapped candy. That's the way the kids get their candy, for they don't hang out socks. When the time came we all walked into the room where the tree was, lit with candles and sparklers, and sang songs. The family opened their presents, then we came back in the kitchen and had dinner of white sausages, a traditional Christmas Eve meal. When we went home there was a surprise waiting for us. Sr. Dzugan, a very sweet professional investigator, very "sympatisch", had left a package for us containing two BU 1970 50 Schilling pieces. R and I lighted the church's tree's candles and opened our presents . . . I opened the package from Darya and found she had knitted me a scarf!

Today for lunch (dinner) we went to the Baumgartners: a wonderful chicken with rice dish, with ice cream for dessert. The latter is unusual for Austria. Sr. Baumgartner is one of the best cooks I have met in Austria, which is saying a lot. In the afternoon we went sledding with the four little kids (Reiter's and Baumgartner's). I wasn't much for it, so after a few times I joined the three real little kids, who had found it too cold, at Sr. Muehlbacher's, who lived right in the area. Afterwards we went to the Baumgartner's, watched a movie, and came home.

At the advice of Pres. Malzl and Sr. Roth, I de-organized the Relief Society to a "Home Relief Society". There simply were not enough active sisters to conduct the entire program. That made Br. R especially mad, as he had been so strong against it. My plans for success here in Braunau are looking good, for I think progress will be made towards a successful conclusion. The next major improvement I am hoping for is Br. R's transfer so as to build unity in the missionary part of the work. I have tried my best to do what I think is right and still preserve his tender feelings, but it seems am unsuccessful at both. It will be rough because everyone likes him here in the branch, and certainly for those who are not trying to accomplish something he has a pleasant personality. I don't know—Es ist ein schwerer Fall.

25 December 1970, Graz

Merry Christmas, Sam!

. . . I'm here in Graz now, and things are looking great. We have golden investigators coming out of our ears. . . I hope things are going great for you there in Braunau. May the Lord bless your efforts with success. . . .

Frodo

25 December 1970, Braunau

Dear Mom & Dad,

. . . It has been a wonderful Christmas . . . I often wish I had a mastery of either German or English so I could at least express my appreciation for God and my family in some language or other. We have been carefully led to our present condition and God's hand has not been held back. . .

I have wanted to tell you about an experience I had many years ago. The winter before we moved back to Portland, at a time when we never supposed we would ever move, I had a dream, not just once, but 3 or 4 times, an unusually vivid dream, the memory of which remains. I dreamt we moved from Sunnyside to Portland, a land I did not care for too much because it was always cloudy and often cold when we visited. We moved to a multi-level house on a hill in my dream, a house painted yellow, a strange color for a house. I attended a school where there was a special window case which seemed to have some meaning. This dream was fulfilled in detail. The significance? If we hadn't moved to Portland we may never have become active in the Church. If we had not moved to that house or a house in that area, we might not have come in contact with the Waddells and the Woods and all the others who have had such good influence on us. I met Don Waddell in that school room with the display window (the Science Room at Dale Ickes Jr. High). Why was I given such a dream? I don't know, except as a personal testimony that God knows us individually, cares about what we do, and influences our lives. And I am sure that as He did it in the past, He will do it in the future. . . .

Love, Rod

Pres. Broberg,

1. My companion takes himself too seriously, excluding the feelings of others in his own missionary attitude.

2. My companion never smiles

3. My companion is not willing to let others make their week as they plan it.

4. He blows up everything twice the size it is or makes it worse than it was in the first place.

5. He is completely opposite from me in interests, etc., but thinks his are the only ones that count.

6. I dislike his attitude from the Sprach Mission (LTM) until this minute.

7. I'm willing to work with him and work it out as soon as he shows me that he is too. Honestly, not like what is wrong with me.

Br. R

I was sorry that we never could reconcile our differences. Certainly it was not all his fault, but it seemed Br. R could never get past my being "*ein kalter Stein*" that Br Welker had mentioned back in the LTM. No doubt I seemed determined to follow the rules as diligently as possible—I was—and no doubt our interests, backgrounds, personalities, and outlooks differed. Those things should not matter—to be effective missionaries, companions have to be united, work together toward their common goals, and cooperate. They don't have to be chums, but they need to be allies.

31 December 1970, Braunau

This evening I said goodbye to Br. R: he was transferred to Vienna. A certain Br. Combs is coming and should arrive in about an hour. It has been an easy week, not accomplishing much. Yesterday we were in Salzburg for District Study Class. It was a good one, all about new programs to be used in the coming year. 1971 will be very good, and I am very happy to write the last lines of the chapter that closed today.

Chapter 12

1 January 1971, Braunau

Dear Mom & Dad,

Happy New Year! Isn't it great? Br. R was transferred to Vienna yesterday. Br. Combs came in his place. Combs has been in Austria since May and is really a nice fellow. It looks fine! All is roses. Last night we walked around the town at midnight in the snow and watched the fireworks. That was fun, as there were a lot of skyrockets, especially in Germany across the river.

. . . We will see some real success in the future. The missionary force here is at an all-time low: 95 missionaries. As far as I know last year produced only about 95-97 baptisms, too. Br. Combs was in pretty close contact with the mission home in *Wien* and said the Pres. is depressed just now, with good reason. He preached Repentance for half an hour to the DLs and ZLs at their conference last week. Depression and negativism are widespread in the mission. The elders have not been doing their job, but neglecting their duty. The mission badly needs to repent.

This is a side of missionary work no one back home sees, because they're so busy hearing the great success reports of other areas. This is neither California nor the Northwest. In Austria no elder is a "baptizing machine". It is arduous, laborious work; house to house, door to door, months with no success, prayers that bring depression because the answer is not seen. And when depression begins, so does negativism; negativism diminishes the little success there is. And so the depression becomes deeper in a vanishing spiral. And what can you do? Only throw yourself upon the mercy of the Lord and repent. Have faith. Be strong. Do what must be done, whether you see success or not, have joy or not—in a phrase: carry on!

So it is in the Austrian Mission as the New Year enters. All have heard the call to repentance. Most have felt it. Many will heed it. The coming year will be exciting here, for much success will be seen as the elders repent. And of course, from a personal stand-point this year has many special meanings. This year is my last in Austria, my last chance to be a successful missionary. In 8 months I will be home. School will start with a new major—Comparative Literature—and a new language—Greek. There will be new friends, and old ones seen again. It will be a good year. The planned high point: a temple ceremony with my parents.

1970 has been good, too. There have been experiences which shall never be forgotten. Frodo and Sam in Wels forged a friendship stronger than any Ring. An unforgettable Summer and Fall were in Reichenhall, a mission paradise. And then new as-signments in preparation for the Great Year of Repentance. . . . 1970 was great! 1971 will be better!

. . . Thanks for the Christmas package. I really needed the socks, and the pajamas are a pleasant and needed surprise. The last of those remarkably good chocolate chip cookies will be eaten at the conclusion of this letter. . .

Love, Rod

6 January 1971, Braunau

Dear Mom & Dad,

. . . Sis. K, one of our members, died Tuesday of a liver ailment. . . The hospitals are Catholic and they hate Mormons. The people from the hospital say she asked to be Catholic again, so they gave her the Last Rites, etc. (This is a well-known tactic here.) Anyway, Br. K, who is very weak in the church, is going along with it. It looks like he'll probably use this as an excuse to apostatize. Then he won't have to feel guilty about not keeping the Word of Wisdom. The other night I went over there to talk about the funeral and he was in a drunken stupor. Br. M, his son-in-law, was smugly happy that I saw it. He's a member, but not friendly to the Church. It is largely his influence which has caused the family to fall away. In any case, it is a real mess. This is the first time in memory that a Mormon in Braunau has died. . .

It has been very cold lately. During the day down to 5 degrees F, and at night to -10 F. The humidity is high, often with fog at night. . . .

Thank you for sending the *Reader's Digest*. It has a lot of very good articles. I'm afraid I'm terribly ignorant of recent history, so a lot of what is said is new to me. The press is so prejudiced and "yellow" here. We just ignore it, or occasionally see a *Newsweek* or *Life*, though the latter is almost as bad as European magazines, just not as dirty.

I take vitamins about every other day. We eat oranges every day now. This winter we should come through pretty well in the sickness dept., though I've a little cold just now. Sickness has really been a problem in the mission in the past and the Pres. is very concerned about ending it: flu shots, good apts with heating, a new rule requiring hats in winter (I can't imagine being without one), etc.

Things are moving right along and we'll be seeing success soon. Please look around for a book in German about the U.S., or better, about Oregon or the Northwest. It would make a good present for the Klingers—they do so much for us. . . . Rod

10 January 1971, Provo

Dear Roderick,

. . . Your Mother said you are branch president now. I'm sure you are having many rewarding experiences. We are having a winter about like 1949. We had a beautiful fall with snow just about a week before the first day of winter. The ground hasn't been bare since. Last week we had zero and below—got down to about 15 below. We had this for about 3 days and nights last week. . . .

Your Mother told me about her baptism when we were there in June. I couldn't help but laugh and cry at the same time. I have always longed for her to be a member. I'm sure this is the result of your good missionary work.

We were so happy they decided to go to the temple and asked us to go with them. . . . We had such a lovely day. We have been back to three sessions since. . . .

Love, Aunt Mildred

It was so cold in Provo that year that BYU almost let the girls wear pants to class. Note the word *almost*. The dress code required skirts or dresses for girls, slacks for boys—no blue jeans. It was nice in Braunau for the first part of the winter, but then turned very cold later, with thick ice. We walked a lot then instead of trying to ride our bikes. News reports had characterized the previous winter as the "worst in central European history"; this year, despite its mild start, they ended up calling it the "coldest in central European history". Some scientists were predicting that we were entering a new ice age.

14 *Jänner* 1971, *Wien*

Dear Elders Saxey and Combs:

Thank you for your very *begeistert* Letters, and I am so very happy to learn that you are happy and that Braunau seems to be on the upward climb. I have always been convinced that when we fully attend our duties, and go forth with that sometimes elusive PMA, we will find good people who will listen to our great message, no matter how difficult the local or area circumstances may be. Braunau just needs two faithful and dedicated Elders like you two, in order to be put in the "Golden *Stadt*" list! Keep up the good work.

With respect to the Aaronic Prieshood Award program. Yes, we do have this in the Mission, and I would be delighted if you emphasized this in your work with the young men in Braunau. It should give them the added incentive to qualify and to receive this recognition at the end of the year. You are on the right track.

May the Lord bless you in your very important and holy callings, to the end that you will find the good people whom He has prepared to receive the Gospel in Braunau. My very best greetings to you and the good members of the *Gemeinde*. Good hunting!

Faithfully your brother, Charles W. Broberg

One of my responsibilities as Branch President was to receive the tithes and offerings of the branch members. These were promptly deposited into an account and transferred to Salt Lake City through the Mission Home. On one occasion I received the tithing and fast offering (money saved on food when fasting) of a sweet widow woman whose meager pension was supplemented by welfare from the Church; I wrote the checks out for her rent each month. I felt guilty receiving her donations, so asked President Broberg about it. "Don't even think about denying her the blessing of paying her tithes and offerings," he said. In the eternal scheme of things the inefficiency of the transaction just did not matter.

15-20 January 1971, Portland

Dear Rod,

. . . We have been snowed in. Monday I went home early because it was snowing so hard. Today I got out for the first time. It was beautiful!! . . . Ed got out with chains, but slipped in the ditch. . . . You sound like they are keeping you busy over there, and it does sound cold. . . . Mom

15 January 1971, Braunau

Dear Mom & Dad,

There are so many things to talk about this week, I don't quite know where to begin. Sr. K was buried Saturday. Br. K let her be buried Catholic, being persuaded by relatives and so forth. He has, as we thought he would, used this as an excuse to apostatize. The priest gave an impersonal and uninteresting talk. The whole affair was a bad joke. We dedicated the grave separately.

In Austria, religion and state are not separate, so to leave a church you just have to fill out a form in the Circuit Court and that's it. Of course, that doesn't affect a person's standing as far as we are concerned, just on the government records. K did that Monday.

We spoke with M, the son-in-law with an evil spirit who is largely responsible for the problems in the family and he invited us back tonight to discuss the church. He hasn't left the church officially yet, but it is coming. It is tense.

Br. K was at Sacrament meeting Sunday and said a few words of thanks to the Branch. We then had a special program introducing some new programs—Home Teaching, Teacher Training, etc. Br. Reiter, the former Branch President whom we are reactivating, was the last speaker and did great! He has made terrific progress the last couple weeks. The last time I spoke with Pres. Broberg he said my assignment was to find someone other than a missionary to be Branch President. I think I've found him.

It is really exciting just now; we've been seeing success proselyting, the brethren accepted their callings as home teachers, we've started a special class for our two deacons to prepare them for priesthood work, etc. Things are working up to a big success. Everything has been improving since Br. R left and Br. Combs came. You've got to have harmony in the companionship first before anything else can succeed.

. . . We went to Salzburg Wednesday for District Meeting. Up at 4:30; bus leaves town square at 5:30. Boom, boom, bounce, bounce, jiggle, jiggle, —ooh! 7:30 am Salzburg train station. Shiver shiver, cold cold, wait wait. Brrr! Brethren come—six in a VW bug—ugh! Study Class—boring, but not too bad. Then back home with the train. Exhaustion.

Pres. Broberg is coming next Tuesday to Salzburg for interviews. It's always great to speak with him, so I'm looking forward to it. Today we're heading over to Simbach across the river to look around, shop, etc. We have been very busy this week and are tired. . . .

Love, Rod

At the bookstore in Simbach I saw a copy of Hitler's book, *Mein Kampf*, on the top shelf. The shopkeeper noticed me, and when I returned a few minutes later the book had been turned around so the title could not be read.

15 January 1971, Klagenfurt

Dear Sax and Combs,

Howdy men! Boy, did I have to hold on to my sides when I heard you two nuts were together! Hey Sax, I heard from Br. Welker this week and he's at the "Y", still with lung problems, but he's got a new car and a wife, almost. He said he'd wait so we could come. He's still studying German and he sounds happy. How's the bike riding? Br. Urbancic is learning respect for icy roads—man, he falls good! . . .

Your Everloving Br. Fager

17 January 1971, Braunau

> *. . . Our friendship with Sr. Dzugan has deepened. She seems to trust me a great deal. Today Br. Olson and Allen were here for a workday and we all went out to her and spoke. She is a very good person and definitely needs our help and a patient ear. Klingers have really been opening up too and we are building a good relationship.*

19 Januar 1971, Ranshofen

Liebe Brüder!

> *Jedes Wort was aus dem Herzen kommt, sucht den Weg zum Herzen Seele. Ich habe mein seelisches Gleichgewicht wieder. Danke unseren Vater dafür! Gespräche mit euch ist Labsal (Trost) für die Seele. Gute Worte haben einen so starken Reflex wie die Lichter des Bäumes auf dieser Karte. Vergleich mit dem letzten Gespräch am Sonntag. Danke, danke, und nochmals danke.*

Eure Sr., Erna Dzugan

(Dear Brethren!

Every word that comes from the heart seeks the way to the heart's soul. I have again my soul-balance. Thanks to our Father! Talks with you are salve for the soul. Good words have so strong a reflection as the lights of the trees on this card. So it was with our last conversations on Sunday. Thank you, thank you, and again thank you.

Your Sister, Erna Dzugan)

22 January 1970, Braunau

Dear Mom & Dad,

. . . How often have you been snowed in now? 3 or 4 times? That is really something. Here in Braunau the winter is passing rather pleasantly—a little snow, but not too cold nor too much. Last night we were at Klinger's and a guy was there who started knocking America, saying we lack energy, have bad highways, etc. I almost cut loose on him, but forebore. Klingers stuck up for us though, and built up the country. If you could send some pictures showing different landscapes, freeways, etc., it could be a good tool to use here.

Tuesday we went to Salzburg for interviews with Pres. Broberg. It was great to talk with him again and he seemed really enthused about Braunau, though we mostly talked about branch finances, which are in serious straits. . .

Sunday we had a workday here with the brethren from Salzburg: Olson and Allen, who is one of my best friends. Towards evening we visited Sr. Dzugan. She is a very good woman about 45 and seems quite frail, almost sickly. She and her husband run a nursery for woodland trees in the forest on the other side of Ranshofen, a nearby town. . . . (S)he gains great strength from the missionaries, though the situation is such that she can't join the Church. . . . It was noticeable last Sunday that she was talking to me the whole time and afterwards the brethren expressed thanks for being able to hear it. It wasn't really a conversation, but rather she just needed someone to talk to, like most people.

Our number one investigator, Leitner, gave us the "X" apparently. The work is going pretty well, though, and we're getting a lot of good contacts with people. The hardest part of the whole thing is trying to get the members to be a little positive about the work . . . That old Positive Mental Attitude is nothing more nor less than Faith itself, and without Faith we can't succeed at anything. Pres. Wood ought to speak to this branch.

We've started eating all three meals here at home like we did in Reichenhall. It is not only 25-50% cheaper, but it's also healthier, not so much grease and fat, etc. Today we had a good concoction of rice and tuna fish (the gourmet kind with spices and vegetables). I like to cook anyway. Klingers are always giving us things—last night a big jar of cranberry preserves. . .

Love, Rod

24 January 1971, Braunau

. . . Last Sunday we held Branch Conference. Sr. Dzugan brought Sr. Jetzlsperger to church. The latter doesn't usually come because of an old feud she has with Sr. Gebauer. The meetings seemed to go well and Sr. J left, apparently none the worse for having come, but two days later she wrote us a letter, scrawled out in uneven letters, that she was leaving the church and contemplating suicide. Why? Because she was not "spared" seeing Gebauer again! Br. Combs was sick, so I called Sr. Dzugan immediately, who went to her. She also had received a letter in which the suicide plan was more explicit. Sr. J. was in a very deep depression. Dzugan has hopefully kept her from drastic action and we will go see her as soon as possible. Sr. J has had a very unfortunate life, lives alone on an isolated farm, and is terribly afraid of people; we are nearly her only contact with the world of people. . . .

Sr. Dzugan is one of the most wonderful people I have ever met. She truly loves people! If our members were as Christian as she is they would be in the celestial kingdom. I do hope she finds a way to join the Church. People like her inspire me to want to do good.

Br. Combs and I have seen much success lately and our programs appear to be bearing fruit. My testimony of Jesus Christ and of the prophet have grown . . .

It is supremely important for us to determine our values and standards and then hold fast to them no matter what. Those values are encompassed by the two great commandments. By loving God we accept His standards and requirements. The second commandment is a little more difficult: How do we love our neighbor? How do we communicate with him? What can we do to break down the barriers between us, especially if that neighbor does not want to help? Love requires patience with weakness until it is overcome in strength; God planted within us the power to change the bitterness of life into sweetness.

25-27 January 1971, Portland

Dearest Rod,

. . . They released me from MIA Secretary job and made me Librarian—this gives me a better chance to be with your Dad at meetings. MIA is just not for a woman with no children at home. . . I will miss working with Marilyn Ward; she's a great person.

. . . All in one month we have had fog, snow, rain, freezing, and yesterday and today gorgeous sunshine—to the point the pussy willows are in bloom, also the Forsythia is starting to bud out. I sure hope we don't lose everything to a freeze now! . . . Mom

29 January 1971, Braunau

Dear Mom & Dad,

. . . We started up a new area, the *Altstadt*. Some of these houses are unbelievable. In the old buildings the stairways are long, narrow, steep, and have no light (certainly no natural light); the ceilings of the stairways are arched, the steps generally of much worn wood and inconsistent in size. Nothing is plumbed, nothing is strait, nothing is level. They are like artificial mountains of brick and wood and mud, in which burrows have been dug. (In other word, not only are many of the people hobbit-size—no joke—but the houses are also hobbit-like.) There is no order in these old houses whatever, and we find ourselves in mazes of corridors and staircases, with doors everywhere and no name plates to distinguish between apartments and bathrooms and storage rooms. . . . Rod

4 February 1971, Mexico City

Dear Weeb,

. . . Edward has Hal all puffed up, as Edward is looking forward to becoming a full-fledged American and is going to join the army and volunteer for service in Vietnam. He says he loves America and is willing to fight for it. He is not going to tell his Mother this until he has made the change. He told Hal about it and they became locked in each other's arms and we were all shedding tears. Edward is a fine boy.

. . . Hal is becoming popular with the new administration in Mexico—In fact is at the statehouse today, having dinner with the new president, whose name is Echeverria—I won't pronounce it for you—he is a wonderful man, and he thinks a lot of Hal, which is ok by me! Hal is becoming well known with his Editorial Page in the *Daily News*, and, by the grace of God, is becoming more favorably know as an editor than he ever could as a concert pianist. . . . Love, Pop

Grandpa Hall always called Mom "Weeb", derived from her middle name, Willoughby. He had moved down to Mexico City at age 80 to live with Hal, Mom's younger brother, and his large family. They had a great time together for a couple years until complications of diabetes became a problem; he eventually was placed in the Union Printers' Home in Colorado Springs, a benefit he had purchased and planned on many years before.

Hal was something of a piano prodigy, able to perform flawless renditions of Beethoven and Chopin in every key, backwards and forwards. It was thought he would have a career as a concert pianist, but the need for work led him to capitalize on his experience growing up in a newspaperman's household and he became editor of the largest English language paper in Mexico. Hal was not always popular with the Mexican government. Years later a different administration decided they had had enough of his pro-Israel stance and forced him into early retirement.

5 February 1971, Braunau

Dear Mom & Dad,

We are finding plenty of people to teach, every day practically. One fellow, Herr Bauer, gave a golden 2nd Discussion. That is the first time I can recall having a really golden 2nd. Golden 1sts and so forth, but not a golden 2nd. We're really hoping to get some baptisms after awhile.

. . . Last week, after two weeks of beautiful sunshine, it turned suddenly cold and in 4 hours we had 4 inches of snow. We now have 6-7 inches. The Austrians are happy—they all claimed it was unhealthy to have such a nice winter. *Naja*. . . . Rod

8 *Febbraio* 1971, *Firenze*

Dear Rod,

. . . The pre-Christmas season found me well and happy in the city of Florence, the old residence of the Italy Mission Home. I was transferred there from *Milano* where I had labored for about seven months. I was blessed with the good fortune of working in the same district as Elder Phillip Stark. How about that!! If Phillip is any worse about answering letters than I, you probably didn't know that bit of news. It was really great to be with him for some time; we worked together in Firenze.

About the 14th of December Phillip was transferred to Venice. He and his companion were the first two missionaries to do the Lord's work in that city. They are really having great success up there now; the people are very friendly and prepared for the gospel! At the same time Phillip went north, I was transferred to *Roma* to be financial secretary of the Mission. I'm still weathering the work alright, but it is sure a lot different than being a full-time "missionary". We are really finding a receptive people here in *Roma* and have a number of really great people on their way to becoming Italian Saints. . . .

While Elder Rector (of the 70) was here for our conferences, he told me that to love someone was to sacrifice for them: Love is sacrifice! He told me that. I believed him, and put it into practice, and I know that he was right. I have never been happier in my life than during these last few months since leaving *Milano* last October. The Lord has been so very good to me, good to us all! We need to always think about His love and sacrifice in order to fulfill our missions in good form.

The Lord is preparing the way before us, you can see it in all that you talk with. Italy, along with the rest of Europe, is beginning to blossom! The Lord wants this people to be gathered and blessed; He is with them and is preparing them for the gospel. All we have to do is live the mission rules and the gospel principles, and He gives them to us to teach and baptize! I love my mission. It's hard work, but I have never found greater satisfaction or happiness! . . .

Love, John

11 February 1971, Braunau

Dear Mom & Dad,

. . . We've had a Chinook wind (*Föhn* in German), so the snow has been melting. It is still a little chilly though and Spring just doesn't come yet in Austria. Things are moving right along for us. . . .

Tuesday we had a particularly good morning. We just went from one contact to another, teaching two hours in two and a half hours of work. How about that! . . . The ZL was here for a workday on Saturday. Br. Graham is the ZL's companion now and it was great to see him again. We worked over in Simbach. . . . Rod

26 February 1971, Braunau

Dear Mom & Dad,

. . . Br. Combs has the flu, so we've been here in the apartment since Tuesday. Oh well, it's good to catch up on reading. . . .

It snowed last night and is snowing now. The wind is really blowing along, too. And we thought Spring was here! Oh well, that's how things are out here on the plains of Mordor.

. . . I just wish we could get people to grow up enough to realize that the Church and Gospel of Jesus Christ are nothing more nor less than helps for us to achieve with, and when we don't use them we harm no one more than ourselves. If we don't keep the commandments and exercise the principles of truth, all we do is retard our own growth and development, no one else's. And if we do hinder someone else, then we're responsible for it and will have to pay in the eternal equalization act. If all men, particularly members of the Church, could just understand that and cease to be children in the things of eternal importance, then there would be peace in every heart. . . .

Love, Rod

From January through April of this year the South Vietnamese, with heavy US air support, made a ground offensive in Laos to disrupt the Ho Chi Minh Trail, the route by which North Vietnamese troops and supplies were secreted into the South. It was an important part of President Nixon's strategy of turning military operations over to the ARVN; though inflicting heavy casualties on the enemy, the campaign was not entirely successful. On 1 March 1971 the Capitol building in Washington was damaged by a protestor's bomb.

Meanwhile, in Austria, we tracted out a group of four pleasant, middle-aged housewives who gather frequently for tea and socializing. They seemed very receptive to the Gospel.

5 March 1971, Braunau

Dear Mom & Dad,

. . . We taught our little group of housewives again. They are quite enthused about the Church and we hope they'll visit us Sunday. . . .

We went over to Klinger's last night and used their record player to play the little message the Church sent out with the new magazine, "*Ensign*". Did you all get that and hear it? It was terrific! If you did not get it yet, do so, it is really great. They had an article about the Jews and Caucasians in Asia which I found most interesting. You know, just the other day I was thinking it should be possible to find traces of the scattering of Israel in Europe on the basis of language, myth, and tradition patterns present in the ancient European cultures. . . .

Thanks for the letter from Grandpa. It sounds like Edward Hall is right on the ball. He was the one we had living with us when Hal visited, wasn't he? That business of volunteering for Vietnam sounds a little radical, but then he isn't the only one toying with the idea. There comes a time when everyone has to stand up for what's right one way or another, and sometimes the available way is "radical" and that's all there is to it.

Tonight is our third Teacher Training Class and I get to give my micro-teaching sample. The last session came off pretty well, and I'm hoping the trend will continue. . . . *Namarie*, Rod

5 *Marzo* 1971, *Roma*

Dear Rod:

It was really great to hear from you and to know that the Lord's marvelous work is strongly going forth in Austria! It's funny how easy it is to forget that there are other missions and thousands of other missionaries throughout the world all finding success and happiness in taking the message of the restored gospel to the needy of this earth. I find myself so involved in our latest challenge or program or what have you that the rest of the world just fades away and all I even want to care about are my contacts and the local branch. I'm sure that you have felt and sensed what I mean. . . .

I've seen it happen all over Italy: a slow baptizing town gets some Elders that know how to work and radiate excitement, the members catch fire, and then baptisms start coming in so fast they don't know how it's happening. The whole secret is a bunch of Elders that won't quit and Elders who can radiate confidence and success and who involve the members in everything they do. It takes "guts", brains, and faith! You've got all the qualifications! Success is guaranteed!

We had a baptism last week and 5 more next Saturday. Oh, Rod, the Lord is truly opening the doors and preparing the way here in Italy! It is so wonderful to see the fruits of your labor and know that you are blessed because you showed the Lord you wanted to work and were willing to pay the price for His help and blessings. . . . I've never been happier. . . .

Love, John

p.s. Tonight *Roma* is having its first real, stick-to-the-ground snowfall!

6 March 1971, Braunau

Jetzlsperger's contemplated suicide was averted, so there is one less problem for now. I am teaching the Teacher Trainer Course here with Sr. Gebauer, Baumgartner, and Reiter. I think we may cancel it though, as things do not seem to be working out well with it. We have assigned Br. B and Br. R to go home teaching with their sons.

Br. Combs has been very concerned with how soon to marry after we get home. The authorities tell us three months after getting home, not more than six! That seems a little fast to me. . . .

7 March 1971, Braunau

Br. Combs celebrated his Hump Day. Time has really flown by. We went to the Konditorei to celebrate.

Today we had investigators at Sunday School—the Dänegger's. Sister Dänegger is one of the group of housewives we have been teaching. Also present were two visitors from Germany and Br. Koetelesch. It all helped to make up for the Baumgartner's absence, who had houseguests. We tried the "Seeding Program", a series of tracts delivered to whole neighborhoods, followed by personal visits. It proved a colossal failure. We are really having difficulty finding things to do at present—tracting Einzelhäuser *in winter is very difficult. It is bitterly cold with lots of snow, in contrast to the mild January we had.*

11 March 1971, Itzehoe

Dear Rod,

N, wie geht's. . . . I really got a kick hearing that John and Phil were together in Florence. . . . That reminds me that Bob Jones is also the mission secretary in Chile. He was a district leader until his call to the office. He said their work has slowed down due to the communistic influence of the new government there. He (said after his mission he) will go to a junior college or to the army as his number is 75 in the draft system. . . .

Our best contact just got real sick with asthma and had to go away for a couple of months so we are looking for more like her. Our other good contact has W of W problems and she doesn't know that we know about them. I sure hope we can bring some of these people around. . . .

Love, Don

12 March 1971, Braunau

Dear Mom & Dad,

Well, another week has ground its way to a halt and I've just gotten up after 10 and a half hours of most welcome sleep. Wednesday was our day to get up at 4:30 (after getting to bed late) to go into Salzburg and yesterday we put in 4 hours of straight tracting followed by member visits—we postponed dinner until we got home later. Anyway, this kid was pretty exhausted.

I guess I sent my long johns and so forth home a little early, as our coldest weather has been in the last two weeks. Snow! And cold! *Hushee Hushee*! But we've been making out okay. Yesterday it snowed and snowed, but today the sun is shining wonderfully, so if we're lucky. . . It was so beautiful in Jan. and Feb., who would have thought of such a ridiculous March?

Today we're planning on going over to Simbach—I am picking up a book I ordered last week, a copy of *Geschichten aus dem Wienerwald*, the play Br. Graham and I saw in Salzburg last summer. Tonight we're going to a World War II movie to celebrate Br. Comb's hump-day.

Wednesday in Salzburg Br. Combs and I gave the Study Class. I had planned it out: "How to be a missionary and be happy anyway." That is trickier than it sounds, though it shouldn't be. Of all people on earth we ought to be happiest, for we are in the service of the living God. And yet, many missionaries aren't, simply because they don't understand what's going on. It proved to be a quite satisfactory discussion up until the end. I had asked Br. R'. to tell us about his happiest experience and tell why it was. Br. R'. is of an opposing philosophy to Br. Combs and myself, and sure enough, what he said didn't fit in at all with what we had all discussed: he tried to shoot us down, but Br. Allen, one of my old Salzburg buddies from Reichenhall days, corrected him. We can forgive Br. R', though he's worrisome. He is green and that is part of the problem, only out about two months. Then too, he's from an all-Mormon town in Idaho. *Ou Weh! Au Weh!* Wouldn't it be great to turn the Mormons into Latter-day Saints?

Sr. Dänegger brought her husband to church Sunday. He was neither impressed nor impressing, though, and apparently thinks we are not old enough to be teaching religion. Therefore, he reckons we must be having trysts with our little group of women here. Apparently the Däneggers have marital problems and his reaction to us is just typical. We'll see what happens. . . .

Love, Rod

p.s. Say, Dad, did you see the Clay-Frazier fight? It was a really good one. We watched it over at Sr. Gebauer's. Boy, are they good fighters! That little Frazier can sure take a beating, can't he?

19 March 1971, Salzburg

Dear Mom & Dad,

. . . This afternoon we ride to Salzburg for a District Conference for the Braunau, Salzburg, Innsbruck, and Vorarlberg branches. Saturday will be a Missionary Zone Conference too, but we will have to be in other meetings. It ought to be good as there have been a lot of transfers since the last conference and we'll be seeing a lot of new faces. The mission is at a low point right now, only 78 missionaries; a lot of greenies will be coming in the next few months.

Apparently Spring has finally come; the past week has been just great. I hope it holds on. I got a letter from Don the other day. He sounds like he's doing okay. It will be great to be together again at the Y next fall. . . .

That's a surprise about Marcie Cantwell getting married. She's just a year younger than I am! You know what some people (including Br. Monson and Rector) tell us?—Get married within three months after our return, six months at the most! . . . "Gettin' kinda radical," says Br. Combs.

Anyway, we gave up the Teacher's Training Course. The people just weren't coming along and it was taking up a lot of our time. Maybe they'll be able to do it again some other time. We've been putting in a lot of work lately, though nothing particularly interesting has happened. A couple kids tried to persecute us, but we went on to the next street. We taught an interesting guy about

65 the other day. When I saw his long, square, grey beard and his brown skullcap I thought he was a Jew (I have yet to talk with one here, though I have met a couple). He turned out to be Catholic. . . . Rod

Joan Rhodes wrote on 21 March that the news said Germany and Austria were having the worst winter in 25 years, despite my writing that it had been mild. The severe weather that year was merely delayed. I had also told her my companion had the *Grippe*, the flu. "Eat well so that you don't get ill. Was that supposed to be a joke about your companion? You once told me that anyone who got sick had the *Grippe* when there was nothing else to call it."

26 March 1971, Braunau

Dear Mom & Dad,

. . . Things are pretty O.K. here. We had conference in Salzburg on Sat. and Sun. We were lucky on Friday to arrive with time to go up in the tram to the fortress on the hill, through the museum, etc. It was really great, something I always meant to do while in Reichenhall. They had a fascinating torture tower. Saturday morning we got to go with Br. Nestlinger on a little tour he gave the BYU student group. We went to Oberndorf, where *Silent Night* was 1st played, then to Arnsdorff, where it was written. The author was a schoolteacher and we saw the desk on which the song was written. There is still a school there and the kids (1st graders) sang the song for us. They also have a bell carillon in the church there and it plays *Silent Night* too. It was a sweet trip.

That afternoon we had meetings with the Mission President, etc. In the evening we had entertainment. Sunday meetings were great. The main meeting was held in the *Mozarteum*, the big music school dedicated to Mozart. It was great to see everybody. Br. Labrum, my LTM companion, and Br. Graham were there, among others. Br. Schubert was made the Branch President of Salzburg and we waited for the Sacrament Meeting to hear him speak, but had to leave too soon. I got to translate for an elderly American gentleman who was there and bore his testimony.

We've been getting a lot of work done. . . I recommended to the President that Braunau be made a dependent Branch (dependent to Salzburg, similar to the relationship between Wels and Linz; that way leadership opportunities for Braunau members will remain, but increased support from Salzburg will free the missionaries to concentrate on missionary work). I think that will be done within a couple months. . . .

Weather has been beautiful the past week and a half. Yesterday it started drizzling, but is still beautiful, a pleasant little rain.

Rod

26 March 1971, Klagenfurt

Servös Sax,

Glad to hear you and Creepy Combs are finding time to tract. Watch that spring fever boys, 'cause it's had me in bed for the last 3 months. Well, I'll have to admit that it's probably 2, or maybe 80% laziness. Ha, chuckle! . . .

Fager

26 March 1971, Graz

Dear Sam,

. . . (I'm the ZL's companion.) We managed to plan it so we used up our Fridays travelling here and there. Since they put me in the car, I have seen Br. Fager a lot more. That guy is really something. He has matured and grown a lot, even lost some more hair. And he has the most baptisms (and most successful) district in the mission (currently tied with Salzburg, though). Anytime Klag can compete with Salzburg, you know things are happening.

We have been really blessed these last couple of months. We have been working hard, contacting or teaching 30 hours a week. We are working with some really cool people now, and I really feel good. Even my health has responded favorably and my attitude has never been better. . . .

Graz has been having a long dry spell in baptisms. Now that our members are finally starting to give *Fuchshofer Briefs*, things should open up. When the missionaries are working hard and the members support us, nothing can stop us from having success.

Well, take care, and we'll see each other again, I hope, before this adventure is over!

Love, Frodo

We did not see each other again—my adventure was almost over.

Chapter 13

On 1 April I received a phone call from President Broberg instructing me to return to Vienna: I was being sent home. The news came as a shock. There was time for only the briefest of goodbyes. I packed and climbed on the train, my mind deep in thought and my heart numb. At the Mission Home that night the mission president sat down with me in his office and explained that the Upper GI report said I had "hepatomegaly". He looked up the word and found it meant "giant liver", which surely meant something serious. He contacted Salt Lake immediately and Elder Monson decided I should be sent home to see doctors there.

President Broberg said my parents had been notified, then asked if I wanted to phone them. Our use of phones had been minimal in Austria and it had not occurred to me that it was possible for me to call home. It was good to hear their voices, but at that point I did not have much to say—I still felt numb. Three weeks passed before I felt up to making another journal entry.

21 April 1971, Portland

The weather turned nice in March and we got a lot of work done. Towards the first of April the pains in my abdomen became worse, so I went to Dr. Muhlbauer, who prescribed some tablets for the gallbladder. I did not respond well to that, so she thought I might have a duodenal ulcer—she sent me to Dr. Melnitzky in Salzburg, who performed an Upper GI series on me and claimed my liver was enlarged and putting pressure on my stomach.

That was Tuesday after District Conference in Salzburg (at which I had spoken with Pres. Broberg and at which Br. Schubert became Branch President). The Dr. recommended I go into the hospital for further examination. Thursday Pres. Broberg called to say he had received a cable from Salt Lake authorizing him to send me home. That night I arrived in Vienna. My traveling companion, also sick, and I left Vienna at 7:30 am Friday and made stops in Munich and Frankfurt before continuing on to New York. In Frankfurt all passengers were frisked to prevent airplane stealing. We separated in New York, where I had a five hour wait. After a 24 hour flight (including the layover), I arrived in Portland at 10:00 pm Friday local time, April 2nd. To my dismay, my dear parents had a wheelchair waiting for me when I arrived. I declined to use it.

Since being home they have done myriad tests on me, including a liver biopsy, for which I had to stay overnight in the hospital. My liver is only a little enlarged, and functions well. They say I have a minor case of post-hepatitic hyperbilirubinemia. Dr. Long, a gastroenterologist, feels I have a disorder of the colon, caused by living conditions and accounting for the pain. Prescription: rest at home and a semi-bland diet.

My status is not yet clarified. President Broberg told me I had "fulfilled" my mission to Austria; Dr. Long recommended against my being returned to work. As yet nothing is resolved and I am officially still on a mission. So at the moment I am neither a missionary nor an RM, and yet both.

My brief hospital stay was uneventful. Dr. Bogaty, one of Dad's friends and employers, performed a bedside needle biopsy of the liver using a spring-loaded biopsy gun. I had two elderly gentlemen as roommates. The next morning as I stood in front of the mirror to finish dressing, I could feel their eyes fixed on me. One commented how easily I was able to tie my tie. Apparently they had not seen a young man in a suit with a white shirt for awhile.

America had a distinctly different atmosphere from when I had left a year and a half earlier. There were coarseness, tension, anger, and a sense of decline that were almost palpable from the moment we touched down in New York. Of course, I had changed during the intervening time, but the country had changed also, and those negative trends and influences that had emerged during the mid and late sixties had become much more widespread.

On 19 April 1971 a week of protests began across the United States, organized by "Vietnam Veterans Against the War". Nearly 200,000 demonstrated in Washington on 24 April. The administration continued drawing down our force in Vietnam, with the last Marine combat unit returning home at the end of April, but the pace of withdrawal was not enough for the protestors. 12,000 were arrested in Washington, D.C., the first week in May.

I used this convalescent period to study and try to be useful in the ward and stake, including joining a ward temple trip by bus to the Oakland Temple, as well as helping Mom and Dad in their callings. There had been some thought of returning to full-time missionary service, but as the weeks passed, it was clear that little time remained for that prior to returning to BYU in the fall. As soon as the release came I was called to serve briefly with the stake young adults. Meanwhile, in Austria, the work went on.

31 May 1971, *Wien*

Dear Elder Saxey:

Thank you so very much for your recent letter, and I hope it has now been fully determined what has caused all your trouble, and the proper treatment has been commenced to restore you to full health and strength.

It was interesting to learn of the new program of missionary work projected for your Ward, and I hope you will be given every opportunity to share your experience with the young people there. Yes, you should surely have more experience in this field than anyone there at home. Have fun and success!

The affairs of the Mission are making progress, but could do much more than at present. There seems to be a fine spirit among the Missionaries, and for the most part they are well and happy. The exceptions are Sister Meyers, who twisted her ankle and now has it in a cast, and will no doubt be sent home to recover because it will take three months to mend. A couple have infected tonsils and allergy problems, but it is all somewhat normal. Our baptisms have not come up to our complete expectations, but we have many fine *Untersuchers*, and I have great hopes for the future. Brother Metzner is now working with Brother Crump in Braunau, and is very happy. We expect to go there next week to meet with the *Geschwister*. (And incidentally the Klingers) They are real fine people, *gel*?

Elder Rector and his wife are coming this week and will hold interviews with the Missionaries here in *Wien*, and also the group from Linz Zone. We start at 6:30 A.M. so you can well imagine it will be a long day. About fifty people.

Now, Dear Brother Saxey, take care of yourself, and I will

be looking forward to a letter from you telling me of your full and complete recovery and restoration to health. It was a real blow to us when you went home, as you were a fine Elder and did an outstanding job as you served your Heavenly Father in this beautiful land. You left legions of friends among the members and your Missionary associates, and have been greatly missed. You have been constantly in our prayers, and we know the Lord is watching over you and has further very important tasks for you to perform. He just wanted you to be well so you could attend to them without interruption.

May the Lord bless you in all your endeavors, and please be assured of my deep thanks and appreciation for the excellent labors you performed as a devoted servant of our Father in Heaven. The Austrian Mission is a better place because of you. Please also express my love and thanks to your parents for the great support they gave us here because of their fine son.

Faithfully your brother, Charles W. Broberg, Mission President

9 July 1971, Vienna

Dear President Emmett (sic, Wood):

We have just been informed by the Church Missionary Committee that Elder Roderick Saxey will not be returned to active missionary work because of the condition of his health, which we exceedingly regret. Because of this we are enclosing Elder Saxey's Honorable Release from this Mission and request that you present it to him with our thanks and appreciation for the excellent labors he performed in the approximate year and a half that he served with us.

Elder Saxey was an outstanding missionary, and in all the

positions of responsibility which he held, he acquitted himself in a splendid way. It was with deep disappointment that we were forced to return him to his home before he had completed his mission . . .

During his mission Elder Saxey had numerous spiritual and faith promoting experiences. It is hope he will be given opportunity to share these with the members of his Ward and Stake. When you see him please give him our love and best wishes for a continuing return to good health. . .

Sincerely your brother, Charles W. Broberg, Mission President

25 August 1971, Portland

I am so sorry I left Austria! I wish I had not gone to the doctor there, and am sure I could have contained the pain until now. Oh, why did I have to get sick and come home? I have thought and thought and wondered why the Lord let that happen to me. Since being home I have read some books, done some yard work, helped out at Chem-Tron, a now defunct plant the family was working on, but accomplished have I nothing.

My mood was very low during this time; I could not help but wonder if I had just complained too much. Had I been a whiner? Church activities and assignments helped fill the days, but only temporarily. Even the prospect of being able to date again was not an entirely happy one. I had written Darya at various times during my mission advising her to date, and she wrote back that she did, but in fact, when I returned to BYU I found that she was waiting, and I sensed that she expected us to pick up where we had left off. I realized though, that my clumsiness with girls was something that needed to be dealt with by socializing, not by going steady. She later married, had children, and, so far as I know, lived happily ever after.

I tried at first to maintain contact with my Austrian friends, but the demands of school, work, and then of family crowded my time, and over the years those contacts were lost: *Das Leben hat mich übernommen.* (Life overtook me.) After finishing a degree in Anthropology, I continued in Pre-medicine, joined the Air Force, and became a physician.

The elevated serum bilirubin that so disturbed the doctors was not "posthepatitic", for I had never had hepatitis. It turned out that all the males in our family have slightly increased bilirubin, a condition known as Gilbert's Syndrome, a genetic disorder in which our livers metabolize bilirubin by an alternate biochemical pathway. It is of no clinical significance other than the confusion it can cause diagnostically. It would have been nice to know prior to going to Austria.

The finding of "hepatomegaly" by the radiologist in Salzburg that so excited President Broberg was completely spurious. Perhaps the doctor had not seen a normal young man's liver shadow lately. The cramping abdominal pain that led to my complaints is best explained as "Irritable Bowel Syndrome", a common disorder aggravated by irregular diet, fatigue, and stress.

In January of 1985 I took the Combat Casualty Care Course in the hills somewhere near San Antonio, Texas. As part of that training we spent an evening in a large field tent watching a lengthy movie taken in Vietnam. These were the military recordings that could not be shown on network TV, but could be shown to a group of doctors, nurses, and medics—this was what our work was all about. The intensity of a firefight with rounds coming from all directions, loading the wounded and dying onto helicopters, patching wounds as they went, was more than could have been anticipated by those of us who had not been on a battlefield. We were in no danger, but our limbs trembled and our eyes moistened; we knew what we were seeing and hearing was real, not make-believe.

One of the major contributors to shell-shock, what later came to be called Post Traumatic Stress Disorder, was the feeling by the patient that he had failed his comrades. His brothers were still in the field while he was at the Aid Station or the hospital or, worse yet, on his way home. There is a sense of guilt, loss, and betrayal, usually subconscious, which greatly undermines the ability to treat physical wounds. It was discovered that whenever possible the "walking wounded", those whose wounds, physical or psychological, were not so severe as to require immediate hospitalization, were best treated by "three hots and a cot". The patient was put to rest for 72 hours and fed good, regular meals, then sent back into the field.

I thought coming home early should have been the missionary equivalent of "three hots and a cot," but the abruptness and completeness of the change left me with a sense of grief, guilt, and failure. There was unfinished business an ocean away. How were Combs, Graham, Allen, Labrum, Fagar, and the rest? What of my good friend Frodo, Br. Duke? And what of the Schuberts, Klingers, Reiters, Darhubers, and all those other dear Austrians; what of Sister Reisenbichler, Sister Rotheneder, Renate Duchet, and Erna Dzugan? I felt an immeasurable loss which has diminished only with the passage of years.

A mission is often referred to as "The Best Two Years". I have had many "best" years since then, studying, marrying, raising children, and serving in various callings and settings. But the passage of time has deepened my appreciation for the mission experience. It was a golden time of youth, faith, and devotion; of intense emotion with great highs and lows, but many more of the former than the latter. That I had the privilege of serving in one of the most beautiful natural settings of the world was a bonus.

But a mission is not just about the missionary and his companions. It was only gradually that I came to understand the sacrifices my parents made for me during this period. The burdens of starting a new business while working full-time, serving in various callings, helping Wayne get started with his family, worrying about Edward, and supporting a missionary, had become great, especially as the new business that they had hoped would provide for their retirement began to fail in 1971. My return home, despite their concern for my well-being, must have been a huge relief to my parents. This was not known to President Broberg, or to Elder Monson, or to me, but the Lord knew, and He takes care of His servants, even in their ignorance. He cares for their families as well. It was important to be with Mom and Dad during this time.

My mission started sweetly in 1969 with Mother's baptism. It was rounded out sweetly in 1971 when Mom and Dad and I knelt around an altar in the Manti Temple and I was sealed to them, child to parents, for time and for all eternity. We had taken the long way to Provo again, visiting Edward and Lynn in California to hear tales of flights and family in faraway places, then driving up through Nevada and Utah to BYU.

It was time for a new adventure.

Chapter 14

Missionaries for the most part are young, still adolescent. Eighteen, nineteen, and twenty year olds on missions have the usual problems and are subject to the usual pitfalls as others their age, hence the importance of following mission rules, obeying the inspired leadership of the mission president and other church leaders, and listening to the guidance of the Holy Spirit at all times. The most important lesson we can learn in this life is how to listen to the Spirit, receive personal revelation, and be obedient to that guidance.

In a sense, every young missionary's story is a "coming of age" story. Normal young men are aware of the pretty girls around them (at some point they may learn that the phrase, "pretty girl" is redundant), and normal young women are equally aware of the boys. Moral purity is an absolute necessity for every missionary—he or she cannot minister without it. Surely there can be no better environment for learning to deal with and to avoid the temptations of sex, including controlling one's thoughts, than while in the Lord's service and in the constant presence of a companion who is equally committed to morality.

To be effective missionaries, it is important to have a unified companionship. Honest, humble communication is paramount. And, as in any close relationship, an extra helping of patience can go a long way. One cannot underestimate how helpful the companionship experience can be as preparation for marriage and family life.

Tracting house to house is very inefficient. We rarely had

referrals, no more than two or three during the entire mission. The most successful missionary work is still by member referral, with member involvement, and member follow-through. As people see the joy the gospel and Church activity bring into their friends' lives they want to be a part of it, and the missionary's task of teaching becomes much easier.

Missionaries need to come into the field prepared intellectually (knowledge of the gospel), spiritually (a testimony of the truth), monetarily (savings to cover as much as possible of their expenses, with plans in place to cover the balance), emotionally (including a good attitude and a genuine desire to serve), and physically. In light of my personal experience, this last point needs elaboration.

The amount of illness we experienced in Austria was not exceptional among missionaries during this time period, and those of us who were sent home for medical reasons constituted a large proportion of returned missionaries. Elders serving in more primitive environments came home early at much higher rates, often with chronic or recurrent diseases that remained with them for the rest of their lives. This did not escape the notice of church leaders.

In 1987 Elder Russell M. Nelson of the Quorum of the Twelve, himself a renowned heart surgeon, called together a group of medical professionals under the direction of Quinton S. Harris, M.D., to form the Missionary Medical Advisory Committee (MMAC). As these began studying the problem they discovered that mission presidents were spending as much as half their time working with sick missionaries; of returned missionaries who had served in developing countries, mostly Latin America, nearly 85% still had some illness even after treatment in the United States.

The committee was able to make a number of recommendations almost immediately, simple steps such as education of missionaries concerning hand washing, water purification, hygiene, safe food preparation, and other disease prevention measures. Onsite evaluation of available medical resources, including local hospitals and clinics, by volunteer American doctors and nurses provided additional guidance for mission presidents and other church leaders. Within the first three years of taking these measures illness among missionaries was reduced by 75%.

After these initial successes, the committee was permanently established and expanded. Physicians were called to serve as Area Medical Advisors, not only in developing countries, but throughout the world. Even missions in Europe and North America were found to have need of education, and medical facilities in need of professional review. Mental and emotional health was considered as well as physical needs. In an article in the *Journal of Collegium Aesculapium* (an association of LDS doctors and other health professionals) in 2006, Dr. Harris reported that 427 physicians and their spouses had served between 1988 and 2005 as Medical Missionaries or Advisors. This work has only increased since that time.

The stress of a full-time mission is far greater than the usual eighteen or nineteen year old has ever experienced; it is more difficult in some respects than boot camp for a military recruit, if for no other reason than it lasts longer. If there is a weakness or predisposition to illness that had gone unnoticed prior to that time, it is likely to emerge on a mission. It is much better to detect a problem and treat it while the candidate is still at home than to send him overseas and have it emerge there, perhaps be mistreated or aggravated, and then need an emergency transfer back. Since establishment of the MMAC the physical, emotional, and mental screening of prospective missionaries has become an essential part of missionary preparation and calling.

It is apparent that many individuals are not physically or emotionally able to serve traditional full-time proselyting missions, despite having great faith and desire to serve. In response to this desire, the Church has expanded the number and scope of Church Service Missions, in which the missionary usually lives at home, serves as little as eight hours per week, and labors in local church facilities including visitors' centers, Institutes, canneries, Deseret Industries, bishops' storehouses, genealogical centers, and other locations. Many render excellent service by working online including performing genealogical work or by telephone answering questions and referring investigators to the proselyting missionaries. The work of salvation is vast and all who can help are invited to do so, each according to the circumstances and talents the Lord has given. To be a part of it is an incomparable joy.

The Church grew more quickly in Austria during the 1970s and 80s. The branch in Salzburg became a ward with the creation of the Salzburg Stake in 1997. Brother Schubert served as the first stake president. Brother Schubert's son, Daniel, became bishop of the Salzburg Ward on 9 October 2011. They still run a resort hotel in Bad Reichenhall.

Felix Nestlinger continued to be a great support to the church in Salzburg and delighted new missionaries and visitors with his tours. In August 1971 he wrote to me, forgetting that I had been there at the time, "You know most probably that we have a new Branch president—Brother Schubert from Bad Reichenhall, so we can say with some conviction that we have a new Bavarian government in the branch."

President Broberg continued in his enthusiastic and positive way. He wrote from his home in California in 1974:

Dear Elder Saxey,

. . . We too are thrilled with the reports of success in Austria and know they are now harvesting much of the seed you fine Elders sowed. We hope to attend the next reunion if the gasoline shortage improves, but if it doesn't, it is extremely *fraglich*. . . .

Your Brother, CW Broberg

He passed away in 1998 at the age of 94.

Frodo completed his mission and returned to being Kent Duke. He graduated in Computer Science from UC Berkeley and became the "Lead Technical Architect" for AT&T. Brother Duke married, had four children, lots of grandchildren, and served in many positions of responsibility in the Church. Now retired, he continues to have great adventures, even skydiving, which is very un-Hobbit.

Erna Dzugan and I exchanged letters through the mid '70s. Life seemed to improve gradually for her. She remained a good friend and helper to Sister Jetzelsperger. In 1972 she wrote, *"Die Liebe, Ich meine die Liebe überhaupt, is doch das grösste Wunder. Sie heilt viele Wunden."* ("Love, I mean, love above all, is the greatest miracle. It heals many wounds.")

Renate Duchet was treated at the LDS hospital in Salt Lake City, met President Joseph Fielding Smith, did very well, and later went to BYU. She taught me the word, *Pfirti*, which is Austrian dialect for "God be with you."

Don Waddell became my roommate again at Deseret Towers, married, and raised a large family of faithful children. His mother's prediction about their cousin living long enough to become the prophet was correct; Thomas Monson became president of the Church in 2008 at the age of 80, still a comparative youngster. Clyde Waddell continued to serve in many positions, eventually as a Stake Patriarch. When he passed away there was standing room only at the funeral service.

Don Wood likewise continued to serve. An interview with him was featured on BYU television about the beginnings of the missionary work in Korea, which stretched back to his graduate student days at Cornell, teaching Brother Kim.

John Smurthwaite loved Italian so much he changed his major. He teaches Latin at a high school in Connecticut. And yes, Italy did lead. By the end of 2012 there were over 24,000 members of the church in Italy, almost five times the number in Austria. President Monson broke ground in 2010 for a temple in Rome.

Mom and Dad served in many callings, including a mission among the Hmong refugee community in Portland, Oregon. They were temple workers in the Portland Temple until their health declined.

Wayne was trained by the army in automotive care and continued learning a variety of skills while raising his young family. He was the kind of man who can do things: fix a car, repair a machine, build a house, whatever needs doing. He later moved back to the Yakima Valley which he loved.

After his tours in Vietnam, Edward stayed in the Naval Reserve until retirement while working as civilian contractor for the Defense Department, specializing in fleet defense. He and Lynn raised four children and now are enjoying their grandchildren. Their youngest, Tom, recently became an Air Force 2nd lieutenant. Good choice of branches, Tom!

As for the war in Vietnam, Richard Nixon was elected and re-elected with the promise that he would extricate us from Johnson's war without turning tail and running—"peace with honor". To accomplish that goal required first an expansion of that part of the war we were most effective at fighting, namely projecting air power by attacking the North in their homeland, their supply routes, and their sanctuaries in Laos and Cambodia. But more importantly, training the South Vietnamese Army (ARVN) as a more effective fighting force became priority one. They had to be able to defend their country without us.

In addition to these military steps, Nixon through his National Security Advisor, Henry Kissinger, initiated secret talks with the mainland Chinese to improve relations with that country and to counter the Soviet Union, North Vietnam's chief supplier, at the same time pursuing a wary standoff with the Soviets called "détente". This series of difficult diplomatic maneuvers eventually bore fruit—a peace treaty went into effect on 28 January 1973, allowing completion of our military withdrawal and the end of the draft.

A year later the North broke the treaty and renewed their attacks on the South. US training had been effective and the ARVN fought valiantly for over two years against a well-supplied enemy. As ammunition began to run out, we were asked to help— as little as 200 million dollars could enable South Vietnam to continue the fight, but Congress, in a cowardly act of political revenge against Nixon, turned them down. This denial of aid led to the South's complete demoralization. Seeing that there was no help coming from America, they fled the battlefield they had been so ably contending. Millions died or became refugees, the famous "boat people", and there was untold suffering.

Over 9 million Americans served in Vietnam, with a peak deployment over 530,000 and more than 58,000 total deaths. Estimates of Vietnamese and other deaths are much higher, probably totaling over two million. Unlike many of the Class of '68, I did not have to go, but the war in which I did participate was not over. Neither was the onward course of history completed.

Exhausted from Vietnam and the continuing Cold War abroad and from social turmoil at home, most Americans only noticed news reports from the Middle East when they were associated with gasoline shortages or American casualties. Few could have imagined what consequence that region would have for us a few decades later. Fewer still could imagine the connections between 20th century events in Europe and our 21st century wars.

It is beyond the scope of this book to explore in detail the intimate links between the Egyptian Muslim Brotherhood and the Nazis, except to mention in passing the devotion of its founder, Al Bana, to Adolf Hitler; or the role of the Brotherhood's Grand Mufti of Jerusalem in recruiting Muslims for a planned "international SS" (he was a frequent visitor to the "Eagle's Nest" in Berchtesgaden and one of the proponents of the Nazis' "final solution" to the "Jewish problem"); or The Brotherhood's training in Saudi Arabia of a young Osama Bin Ladin. Thus the threads of history overlap and interweave. As World War I led to World War II, so the seeds of our 21st century wars in the Middle East were sown in the first half of the 20th.

America in the mid-1970s was re-grouping from a period of rapid change and surprising defeat. Our attempted withdrawal from the world did not last long. In far away Iran (ancient Persia) the imprisoned rebel cleric, Ruhollah Khomeini, later given the title *Ayatollah*, was developing a concept of government in which Muslim religious leaders would act as "guardians" not only of the government, but of all individuals in the conduct of their daily lives. Perhaps he did not know how closely he was re-working the thoughts of Lenin, Hitler, and Mao and casting them in an Islamic religious mold, or how closely all such ideologies of force and co-ercion are modeled on the original plan of Satan introduced in the War in Heaven so long ago, denying our agency. Khomeini is dead now. I suppose someone in the Spirit World has filled him in.

No power or influence

can or ought to be maintained

by virtue of the priesthood,

only by persuasion, by long-suffering,

by gentleness and meekness,

and by love unfeigned;

by kindness, and pure knowledge,

which shall greatly enlarge the soul

without hypocrisy, and without guile.

D & C 121: 41-42

Appendix I: Glossary

Altstadt	old town
	(In America this usually means a street or two of 19th century buildings, in Austria they are Medieval.)
auf Englisch	in English
Aufmarsch	parade
aber	but
Apfelsaft	apple juice
Ausländer	foreigner
Bahnhof	train station
besonders	particularly, specially
Bauernhof, Bauernhöfe	farmhouse, farmhouses
	(These are often elaborate compounds with room for farm animals and a central courtyard.)
begeistert	enthused, enthusiastic
Bezirk	district, borough
Bis Später	'til later (We would say, "See you later.")
Brief	letter

D&C	*Doctrine and Covenants*
	(A collection of scriptures given by revelation through Joseph Smith and his successors.)
Deutsch	German
Donau	Danube
ein kalter Stein	a cold stone
Einzelhäuser	single family houses
Es ist ein schwerer Fall.	It is a difficult case.
FHE	Family Home Evening
	(Members of the Church are encouraged to gather their families together once a week for a spiritual lesson or message, often with games and refreshments.)
fraglich	questionable, doubtful
Freie Rede Lehrerin	conversation teacher
Freude	joy
freuen auf	looking forward to
Frohe Weihnachten!	Merry Christmas!
Fuchshofer Brief	Brother Fuchshofer wrote a powerful testimony in the form of a letter which members could use to introduce

	friends and family to the Gospel.
Gasthaus	inn
gel	agreed? (dialect)
Gemeinde	community, parish, an LDS Church branch or ward
Gemeindevorsteher	branch president, leader
Geschichten aus dem Wiener Wald	
	Tales From the Vienna Woods
Geschwister	brothers and sisters
	(One word instead of three— isn't German great!)
Gott sei mit dir!	God be with you!
Grippe	the flu
Hauptbahnhof	main train station
Jänner	alternate form of *Januar* (January)
Jedermann	Everyman
	(*Jedermann* is a play by Austrian playwright Hugo von Hofmannsthal, based on a 15th century English morality play. The story is of a rich man who approaches death and judgment with the devil waiting for him, but is saved

	by faith, good works, and the grace of Jesus Christ.)
kaput	kaput
Kirchensteuer	church tax
Körper	body
Liebe Eltern	Dear Parents
Lebkuchen	gingerbread cookies
LTM	Language Training Mission, *Sprachmission* in German
Namarie	farewell (Tolkien's "Elvish")
N, wie geht's	How's it going?
	(The "N" at the beginning is a colloquial, conversational interjection, probably meaning "So . . .")
PMA	Positive Mental Attitude
Naja	Oh, well.
RM	Returned Missionary
Schicken	to send
sämtliche alte verückte Weiben	(a group of) crazy old ladies
	(Not a very kind thing to say. The discussion in the text to seeing a dog refers to a popular TV advertisement of the time.)

Schönbrunn	The imperial palace in Vienna; literally, "beautiful fountain or spring."
Schöne Gruss (Grüsse)	Greetings! Literally, beautiful greetings
Stadt	city or town
Stadtplatz	town square
Staatstheater	national theater
	(The *Staatstheater* in Vienna is one of the great operatic venues of the world, comparable to the Metropolitan Opera in New York City.)
Stake	An ecclesiastical unit about the size of a diocese, consisting of several wards.
Stiega	apartment house
Untersuchers	investigators
Versand	shipment or dispatch
Viel'n Glück!	Good luck!
Vortrag	presentation, lecture
Ward	A local congregation like a parish, 100-600 people, presided over by a bishop.
wegen	because of
Ach, Weh! Ou, Weh! Au, Weh!	Oh, the pain!

Wohnung	home, dwelling place
Word of Wisdom	The principles of health taught in the Church and required for temple attendance.
Wie, bitte?	"What did you say? Come again?" Literally, "how, please?"
Wunderbar	wonderful
Zuhörer	listeners, audience
zum bügel'n	for pressing or ironing (clothing)

Appendix II: Selected Bibliography

Missionary Health:

Harris, Quinton S., M.D. "Called to Serve: A History of the Health Division of the Missionary Department", *Journal of Collegium Aesculapium*, 2006. P22-25

"Health and the Missionary", *The Ensign*, Feb 1991

The Church in Austria:

http://www.mormonnewsroom.org/facts-and-statistics/country/austria

About Felix Nestlinger:

http://news.google.com/newspapers?nid=336&dat=19740504&id=uKZSAAAAIBAJ&sjid=LX8DAAAAIBAJ&pg=4424,1365857

About President Broberg:

http://www.deseretnews.com/article/628721/Death--Charles-W-Todd-Broberg.html?pg=all

"Neues aus Österreich" - 17 September 2011:

http://www.hlt.at/nc/nachrichten/artikelansicht/archive/2011/september/article/jubilaeumsfeiern-anlaesslich-30-jahre-kirchengebaeude-in-salzburg.html?cHash=5a166856a1&print=1

"The Church in Europe", *The Ensign*, August 1973

Missionary Work in The 1960s-1970s:

Richards, Franklin D., "Share the Gospel", *Conference Report*, April 1961, pp. 83-87

Hinckley, Gordon B., "Ready to Harvest", *Conference Report*, April 1961, pp. 87-90

History of the Uniform System of Teaching:

http://maxwellinstitute.byu.edu/publications/books/?bookid=47&chapid=266

The War in Vietnam:

http://www.uscarriers.net/cv66history.htm

http://www.uscarriers.net/cvn65history.htm

http://www.cbsnews.com/8301-18563_162-57556318/tragedy-remembered-as-uss-enterprise-is-retired/

http://www.historyplace.com/unitedstates/vietnam/

http://www.amervets.com/warlib6/warlib6v.htm

Other events of the 1960s-1970s and related items:

Conditions in 1968, with follow up on some of the troublemakers:

http://www.nationalreview.com/article/352753/vignette-68-revolutionaries-revisited-m-d-aeschliman

Estimates of casualties due to communism:

http://www.battleswarmblog.com/?p=1191

History of Earth Day:

http://spectator.org/archives/2013/04/22/happy-earth-day-and-lenin-day

There are many discussions of the relationship between radical Islam and the Nazis. Here is one:

http://www.canadafreepress.com/2006/loftus101106.htm

History and controversy of Hitler's birthplace:

http://www.dw.de/was-tun-mit-hitlers-geburtshaus/a-16829275

Austria during WWII:

http://www.dw.de/österreichs-rolle-in-der-ns-zeit/a-16662912

Professor Nibley's wartime and missionary experiences:

Nibley, Hugh, and Nibley, Alex, *Sergeant Nibley, Ph.D.: Memories of an Unlikely Screaming Eagle*, Deseret Book, 2006

Illustrations

Like our memories, many have inadequate resolution and are blurred, but are as dear as those which are crisp and clear.

The Waddells in 1967

Mom and Dad Saxey in Portland

Wayne in 1961

Edward with his F4 aboard the *USS Enterprise*

Bremen District: Welker, Olson, Duke, Patten, Labrum, Perry, Hirst

John Smurthwaite at LTM

Wels, a recent picture

Br. Archibald in front of the door to our Wels apartment

The Zwiebelturm in Wels

Me, studying while sick in Wels

Br. Fagar shortly before transfer

May Day parade in Wels

Helping Br. Eidherr tear down an old farmhouse

Sr. Reisenbichler with Br. Duke

The Wels Branch

Salzburg with Untersberg in the background, a recent picture

Hallstatt in the Salzkammergut, a recent picture

Gosau in the Salzkammergut, a recent picture

Br. Nestlinger and me

Br. Nestlinger and friends

Br. Graham and Br. Nestlinger

Renate Duchet with missionaries

Berchtesgaden, a recent picture

Bad Reichenhall town square, a recent picture

Br. Graham in Berchtesgaden

Missionaries in Innsbruck

All Enlisted

Innsbruck

Innsbruck, a recent picture

The Schuberts in Bad Reichenhall

Missionary Breakfast

Salzburg seen from the fortress, a recent picture

Braunau am Inn, a recent picture

Braunau from the bridge over the river Inn

Br. Combs in front of a Stiega

Sr. Dzugan with her son and daughter

Don Waddell in 1971 at Itzehoe

Lynn and Edward in 1971

Me in 1971

Salzburg in summer, a recent picture

Salzburg in winter, a recent picture

Made in the USA
San Bernardino, CA
09 December 2014